Andrew Carnegie

ANDREW CARNEGIE'S OWN STORY

Reprinted for
THE CARNEGIE DUNFERMLINE TRUST
By kind permission of
HOUGHTON MIFFLIN COMPANY
BOSTON AND NEW YORK

This book comprises a series of chapters from *The Autobiography of Andrew Carnegie* condensed by Eva March Tappan, Ph.D.

This edition (Illustrated) 1984

ISBN 0 947559 02 7 (Hardback)

ISBN 0 947559 01 9 (Paperback)

Printed in Scotland
by HOLMES MCDOUGALL LIMITED, EDINBURGH

FOREWORD

JUST as my mother in 1920 wrote the preface to the 'Autobiography of Andrew Carnegie', I am very glad to be associated with this new edition of the shortened form of his own story. I hope it will be enjoyed by all who read it, especially those who know and love the auld grey toun where he was a boy.

Although my father left Scotland when he was 12 years of age, he talked to me a great deal about Dunfermline, where he had been born; and I can remember standing with him on a rock in Pittencrieff Glen in Dunfermline and reciting the first verses of *The Ballad of Sir Patrick Spens:*—

'The King sits in Dunfermline tower*
Drinking the bluid-red wine . . .'

with the altered *happy* ending that Daddy had written for the sad tale —

'The sun shone bright on the Abbey walls
When they landed at Aberdour
With the fairest bride that ever was seen
By the King in Dunfermline Tower.'

My father thoroughly enjoyed life. He enjoyed his work and what his wealth brought him, and he greatly enjoyed giving it away. But he did not just throw money away: the other party had to do their share — for instance, if people got an organ or a public library they had to promise to meet the running costs.

I would like to have him remembered for his buoyancy, for his zest in life, and for his desire that everybody who could possibly do so would share in the good things in life and the joy of putting their own effort into it as well as receiving from it.

MARGARET CARNEGIE MILLER

* Mr. Carnegie preferred 'tower' to the more usual 'toun'.

PREFACE

TO THE COMPLETE EDITION OF THE AUTOBIOGRAPHY

AFTER retiring from active business my husband yielded to the earnest solicitations of friends, both here and in Great Britain, and began to jot down from time to time recollections of his early days. He soon found, however, that instead of the leisure he expected, his life was more occupied with affairs than ever before, and the writing of these memoirs was reserved for his play-time in Scotland. For a few weeks each summer we retired to our little bungalow on the moors at Aultnagar to enjoy the simple life, and it was there that Mr. Carnegie did most of his writing. He delighted in going back to those early times, and as he wrote he lived them all over again. He was thus engaged in July, 1914, when the war clouds began to gather, and when the fateful news of the 4th of August reached us, we immediately left our retreat in the hills and returned to Skibo to be more in touch with the situation.

These memoirs ended at that time. Henceforth he was never able to interest himself in private affairs. Many times he made the attempt to continue writing, but found it useless. Until then he had lived the life of a man in middle life — and a young one at that — golfing, fishing, swimming each day, sometimes doing all three in one day. Optimist as he always was and tried to be, even in the face of the failure of his hopes, the world disaster was too much. His heart was broken. A severe attack of influenza followed by two serious attacks of pneumonia precipitated old age upon him.

PREFACE

It was said of a contemporary who passed away a few months before Mr. Carnegie that "he never could have borne the burden of old age." Perhaps the most inspiring part of Mr. Carnegie's life, to those who were privileged to know it intimately, was the way he bore his "burden of old age." Always patient, considerate, cheerful, grateful for any little pleasure or service, never thinking of himself, but always of the dawning of the better day, his spirit ever shone brighter and brighter until "he was not, for God took him."

Written with his own hand on the fly-leaf of his manuscript are these words: "It is probable that material for a small volume might be collected from these memoirs which the public would care to read, and that a private and larger volume might please my relatives and friends. Much I have written from time to time may, I think, wisely be omitted. Whoever arranges these notes should be careful not to burden the public with too much. A man with a heart as well as a head should be chosen."

Who, then, could so well fill this description as our friend Professor John C. Van Dyke? When the manuscript was shown to him, he remarked, without having read Mr. Carnegie's notation, "It would be a labor of love to prepare this for publication." Here, then, the choice was mutual, and the manner in which he has performed this "labor" proves the wisdom of the choice — a choice made and carried out in the name of a rare and beautiful friendship.

LOUISE WHITFIELD CARNEGIE

CONTENTS

CHAPTER I

A LITTLE SCOTCH BOY

I WAS born in Dunfermline, in the attic of the small one-story house, corner of Moodie Street and Priory Lane, on the 25th of November, 1835, and, as the saying is, "of poor but honest parents, of good kith and kin." Dunfermline had long been noted as the center of the damask trade in Scotland. My father, William Carnegie, was a damask weaver, the son of Andrew Carnegie after whom I was named.

My Grandfather Carnegie, born in Patiemuir, two miles from Dunfermline, was well known throughout the district for his wit and humor, his genial nature and irrepressible spirits. He was head of the lively ones of his day, and known far and near as the chief of their joyous club—"Patiemuir College." Upon my return to Dunfermline, after an absence of fourteen years, I remember being approached by an old man who had been told that I was the grandson of the "Professor," my grandfather's title among his cronies. He was the very picture of palsied eld;

"His nose and chin they threatened ither."

As he tottered across the room toward me and laid his trembling hand upon my head he said: "And ye are the grandson o' Andra Carnegie! Eh, mon, I ha'e seen the day when your grandfaither and I could ha'e hallooed ony reasonable man oot o' his jidgment."

Several other old people of Dunfermline told me stories of my grandfather. Here is one of them:

One Hogmanay night, a time of merriment and practical jokes, an old wifey, quite a character in the village, being surprised by a disguised face suddenly thrust in at the window, looked up and after a moment's pause exclaimed, "Oh, it's jist that daft callant Andra Carnegie." She was right; my grandfather at seventy-five was out frightening his old lady friends, disguised like other frolicking youngsters.

I think my optimistic nature, my ability to shed trouble and to laugh through life, making "all my ducks swans," as friends say I do, must have been inherited from this delightful old masquerading grandfather whose name I am proud to bear. A sunny disposition is worth more than fortune. Young people should know that it can be cultivated; that the mind like the body can be moved from the shade into sunshine. Let us move it then. Laugh trouble away if possible.

On my mother's side the grandfather was even more marked, for my Grandfather Thomas Morrison was a born orator, a keen politician, and the head of the advanced wing of the radical party in the district. More than one well-known Scotsman in America has called upon me, to shake hands with "the grandson of Thomas Morrison."

My Grandfather Morrison married Miss Hodge, of Edinburgh, a lady in education, manners, and position, who died while the family was still young. At this time he was in good circumstances, a leather merchant conducting the tanning business in Dunfermline; but the peace after the Battle of Waterloo involved him in ruin, as it did thousands; so that while my Uncle Bailie, the eldest son, had been brought up in what might be termed luxury, for he had a pony to ride, the younger members of the family encountered other and harder days.

The second daughter, Margaret, was my mother, about whom I cannot trust myself to speak at length. She inherited from her mother the dignity, refinement, and air of the cultivated lady. Perhaps some day I may be able to tell the world something of this heroine, but I doubt it. I feel her to be sacred to myself and not for others to know. None could ever really know her—I alone did that. After my father's early death she was all my own. The dedication of my first book, *An American Four-in-Hand in Great Britain* (New York, 1888), tells the story. It was: "To my favorite Heroine My Mother."

Fortunate in my ancestors I was supremely so in my birthplace. Where one is born is very important, for different surroundings and traditions appeal to and stimulate different latent tendencies in the child. Ruskin truly observes that every bright boy in Edinburgh is influenced by the sight of the Castle. So is the child of Dunfermline, by its noble Abbey, the Westminster of Scotland, founded early in the eleventh century (1070) by Malcolm Canmore and his Queen Margaret, Scotland's patron saint. The ruins of the great monastery and of the Palace where kings were born still stand, and there, too, is Pittencrieff Glen, embracing Queen Margaret's shrine and the ruins of King Malcolm's Tower, with which the old ballad of "Sir Patrick Spens" begins:

> "The King sits in Dunfermline *tower*,[1]
> Drinking the bluid red wine."

---

[1] *The Percy Reliques* and *The Oxford Book of Ballads* give "town" instead of "tower"; but Mr. Carnegie insisted that it should be "tower."

The tomb of The Bruce is in the center of the Abbey, Saint Margaret's tomb is near, and many of the "royal folk" lie sleeping close around. Fortunate, indeed, the child who first sees the light in that romantic town, which occupies high ground three miles north of the Firth of Forth, overlooking the sea, with Edinburgh in sight to the south, and to the north the peaks of the Ochils clearly in view. All is still redolent of the mighty past when Dunfermline was both nationally and religiously the capital of Scotland.

As my father succeeded in the weaving business we removed from Moodie Street to a much more commodious house in Reid's Park. My father's four or five looms occupied the lower story; we resided in the upper, which was reached, after a fashion common in the older Scottish houses, by outside stairs from the pavement. It is here that my earliest recollections begin, and, strangely enough, the first trace of memory takes me back to a day when I saw a small map of America. It was upon rollers and about two feet square. Upon this my father, mother, Uncle William, and Aunt Aitken were looking for Pittsburgh and pointing out Lake Erie and Niagara. Soon after my uncle and Aunt Aitken sailed for the land of promise.

The change from hand-loom to steam-loom weaving was disastrous to our family. My father did not recognize the impending revolution, and was struggling under the old system. His looms sank greatly in value, and it became necessary for that power which never failed in any emergency—my mother—to step forward and endeavour to repair the family fortune. She opened a small shop in Moodie Street and contributed to the revenues which, though slender, nevertheless at that time sufficed to keep us in comfort and "respectable."

I remember that shortly after this I began to learn what poverty meant. Dreadful days came when my father took the last of his webs to the great manufacturer, and I saw my mother anxiously awaiting his return to know whether a new web was to be obtained or that a period of idleness was upon us. We were not, however, reduced to anything like poverty compared with many of our neighbors. I do not know to what lengths of privation my mother would not have gone that she might see her two boys wearing large white collars, and trimly dressed.

In an incautious moment my parents had promised that I should never be sent to school until I asked leave to go. This promise I afterward learned began to give them considerable uneasiness because as I grew up I showed no disposition to ask. The schoolmaster, Mr. Robert Martin, was applied to and induced to take some notice of me. He took me upon an excursion one day with some of my companions who attended school, and great relief was experienced by my parents when one day soon afterward I came and asked for permission to go to Mr. Martin's school. I need not say the permission was duly granted. I had then entered upon my eighth year.

The school was a perfect delight to me, and if anything occurred which prevented my attendance I was unhappy. This happened every now and then because my morning duty was to bring water from the well at the head of Moodie Street. The supply was scanty and irregular. Sometimes it was not allowed to run until late in the morning and a score of old wives were sitting around, the turn of each having been previously secured through the night by placing a worthless can in the line. This, as might be expected, led to numerous contentions in which I would not be put down even by these venerable old dames. I earned the reputation of being "an awfu' laddie."

In the performance of these duties I was often late for school, but the master, knowing the cause, forgave the lapses. In the same connection I may mention that I had often the shop errands to run after school, so that in looking back upon my life I have the satisfaction of feeling that I became useful to my parents even at the early age of ten. Soon after that the accounts of the various people who dealt with the shop were entrusted to my keeping so that I became acquainted, in a small way, with business affairs even in childhood.

One cause of misery there was, however, in my school experience. The boys nicknamed me "Martin's pet," and sometimes called out that dreadful epithet to me as I passed along the street. I did not know all that it meant, but it seemed to me a term of the utmost opprobrium, and I know that it kept me from responding as freely as I should otherwise have done to that excellent teacher, my only schoolmaster, to whom I owe a debt of gratitude which I regret I never had opportunity to do more than acknowledge before he died.

I may mention here a man whose influence over me cannot be overestimated, my Uncle Lauder. My father was necessarily constantly at work in the loom shop and had little leisure to bestow upon me through the day. My uncle being a shopkeeper in the High Street was not thus tied down. Note the location, for this was among the shopkeeping aristocracy, and high and varied degrees of aristocracy there were even among shopkeepers in Dunfermline. Deeply affected by my Aunt Seaton's death, which occurred about the beginning of my school life, he found his chief solace in the companionship of his only son, George, and myself. He possessed an extraordinary gift of dealing with children and taught us many things. Among others I remember how he taught us British history by imagining each of the monarchs in a certain place upon the walls of the room performing the act for which he was well known. Thus for me King John sits to this day above the mantelpiece signing the Magna Charta, and Queen Victoria is on the back of the door with her children on her knee.

It was from my uncle I learned all that I know of the early history of Scotland—of Wallace and Bruce and Burns, of Blind Harry's history, of Scott, Ramsay, Tannahill, Hogg, and Fergusson. I can truly say in the words of Burns that there was then and there created in me a vein of Scottish prejudice (or patriotism) which will cease to exist only with life. Wallace, of course, was our hero. Everything heroic centered in him. Sad was the day when a wicked big boy at school told me that England was far larger than Scotland. I went to the uncle, who had the remedy.

"Not at all, Naig; if Scotland were rolled out flat as England, Scotland would be the larger, but would you have the Highlands rolled down?"

Oh, never! There was balm in Gilead for the wounded young patriot. Later the greater population of England was forced upon me, and again to the uncle I went.

"Yes, Naig, seven to one, but there were more than that odds against us at Bannockburn." And again there was joy in my heart—joy that there were more English men there since the glory was the greater.

Uncle Lauder has told me since that he often brought people into the room assuring them that he could make

"Dod" (George Lauder) and me weep, laugh, or close our little fists ready to fight—in short, play upon all our moods through the influence of poetry and song. The betrayal of Wallace never failed to cause our little hearts to sob, a complete breakdown being the invariable result. Often as he told the story it never lost its hold. How wonderful is the influence of a hero upon children!

I spent many hours and evenings in the High Street with my uncle and "Dod," and thus began a lifelong brotherly alliance between the latter and myself. "Dod" and "Naig" we always were in the family. I could not say "George" in infancy and he could not get more than "Naig" out of Carnegie, and it has always been "Dod" and "Naig" with us. No other names would mean anything.

There were two roads by which to return from my uncle's house in the High Street to my home in Moodie Street at the foot of the town, one along the eerie churchyard of the Abbey among the dead, where there was no light; and the other along the lighted streets by way of the May Gate. When it became necessary for me to go home, my uncle, with a wicked pleasure, would ask which way I was going. Thinking what Wallace would do, I always replied I was going by the Abbey. I have the satisfaction of believing that never, not even upon one occasion, did I yield to the temptation to take the other turn and follow the lamps at the junction of the May Gate. I often passed along that churchyard and through the dark arch of the Abbey with my heart in my mouth. Trying to whistle and keep up my courage, I would plod through the darkness, falling back in all emergencies upon the thought of what Wallace would have done if he had met with any foe, natural or supernatural.

Andrew Carnegie's mother.

'Uncle Lauder' (George Lauder Snr.) with his wife.

The weaver's cottage, Moodie Street, Dunfermline, in which Andrew Carnegie was born in 1835.

Dunfermline Abbey in 1650.

CHAPTER II

COMING TO AMERICA

MY good Uncle Lauder justly set great value upon recitation in education, and many were the pennies which Dod and I received for this. In our little frocks or shirts, our sleeves rolled up, paper helmets and blackened faces, with laths for swords, my cousin and myself were kept constantly reciting Norval and Glenalvon, Roderick Dhu and James Fitz-James to our schoolmates and often to the older people.

My power to memorize must have been greatly strengthened by the mode of teaching adopted by my uncle. I cannot name a more important means of benefiting young people than encouraging them to commit favorite pieces to memory and recite them often. Anything which pleased me I could learn with a rapidity which surprised partial friends. I could memorize anything whether it pleased me or not, but if it did not impress me strongly it passed away in a few hours.

One of the trials of my boy's life at school in Dunfermline was committing to memory two double verses of the Psalms which I had to recite daily. My plan was not to look at the psalm until I had started for school. It was not more than five or six minutes' slow walk, but I could readily master the task in that time, and, as the psalm was the first lesson, I was prepared and passed through the ordeal successfully. Had I been asked to repeat the psalm thirty minutes afterwards the attempt would, I fear, have ended in disastrous failure.

The first penny I ever earned or ever received from

any person beyond the family circle was one from my school-teacher, Mr. Martin, for repeating before the school Burns's poem, "Man was made to Mourn." In writing this I am reminded that in later years, dining with Mr. John Morley in London, the conversation turned upon the life of Wordsworth, and Mr. Morley said he had been searching his Burns for the poem to "Old Age," so much extolled by him, which he had not been able to find under that title. I had the pleasure of repeating part of it to him. He promptly handed me a second penny.

One of the chief enjoyments of my childhood was the keeping of pigeons and rabbits. I am grateful every time I think of the trouble my father took to build a suitable house for these pets. Our home became headquarters for my young companions. My mother was always looking to home influences as the best means of keeping her two boys in the right path. She used to say that the first step in this direction was to make home pleasant; and there was nothing she and my father would not do to please us and the neighbors' children who centered about us.

My first business venture was securing my companions' services for a season as an employer, the compensation being that the young rabbits, when such came, should be named after them. The Saturday holiday was generally spent by my flock in gathering food for the rabbits. My conscience reproves me to-day, looking back, when I think of the hard bargain I drove with my young playmates, many of whom were content to gather dandelions and clover for a whole season with me, conditioned upon this unique reward—the poorest return ever made to labor. Alas! what else had I to offer them! Not a penny.

I treasure the remembrance of this plan as the earliest evidence of organizing power upon the development of which my material success in life has hung—a success not to be attributed to what I have known or done myself, but to the faculty of knowing and choosing others who did know better than myself. Precious knowledge this for any man to possess. I did not understand steam machinery, but I tried to understand that much more complicated piece of mechanism—man. Stopping at a small Highland inn on our coaching trip in 1898, a gentleman came forward and introduced himself. He was Mr. MacIntosh, the great furniture manufacturer of Scotland—a fine character as I found out afterward. He said he had ventured to make himself known as he was one of the boys who had gathered spoil for the rabbits, and had "one named after him." It may be imagined how glad I was to meet him—the only one of the rabbit boys I have met in after-life.

With the introduction and improvement of steam machinery, trade grew worse and worse in Dunfermline for the small manufacturers, and at last a letter was written to my mother's two sisters in Pittsburgh stating that the idea of our going to them was seriously entertained—not, as I remember hearing my parents say, to benefit their own condition, but for the sake of their two young sons. Satisfactory letters were received in reply. The decision was taken to sell the looms and furniture by auction. And my father's sweet voice sang often to mother, brother, and me:

> "To the West, to the West, to the land of the free
> Where the mighty Missouri rolls down to the sea;
> Where a man is a man even though he must toil
> And the poorest may gather the fruits of the soil."

The proceeds of the sale were most disappointing. The looms brought hardly anything, and the result was that twenty pounds more were needed to enable the family to pay passage to America. Here let me record an act of friendship performed by a lifelong companion of my mother—who always attracted stanch friends because she was so stanch herself—Mrs. Henderson, by birth Ella Ferguson, the name by which she was known in our family. She boldly ventured to advance the needful twenty pounds, my Uncles Lauder and Morrison guaranteeing repayment. Uncle Lauder also lent his aid and advice, managing all the details for us, and on the 17th day of May, 1848, we left Dunfermline. My father's age was then forty-three, my mother's thirty-three. I was in my thirteenth year, my brother Tom in his fifth year—a beautiful white-haired child with lustrous black eyes, who everywhere attracted attention.

I had left school forever, with the exception of one winter's night-schooling in America, and later a French night-teacher for a time, and, strange to say, an elocutionist from whom I learned how to declaim. I could read, write, and cipher, and had begun the study of algebra and of Latin. A letter written to my Uncle Lauder during the voyage, and since returned, shows that I was then a better penman than now. I had wrestled with English grammar, and knew as little of what it was designed to teach as children usually do. I had read little except about Wallace, Bruce, and Burns; but knew many familiar pieces of poetry by heart. I should add to this the fairy tales of childhood, and especially the "Arabian Nights," by which I was carried into a new world. I was in dreamland as I devoured those stories.

On the morning of the day we started from beloved Dunfermline, in the omnibus that ran upon the coal railroad to Charlestown, I remember that I stood with tearful eyes looking out of the window until Dunfermline vanished from view, the last structure to fade being the grand and sacred old Abbey. During my first fourteen years of absence my thought was almost daily, as it was that morning, "When shall I see you again?" Few days passed in which I did not see in my mind's eye the talismanic letters on the Abbey tower—"King Robert The Bruce." All my recollections of childhood, all I knew of fairyland, clustered around the old Abbey and its curfew bell, which tolled at eight o'clock every evening and was the signal for me to run to bed before it stopped.

Father and mother, sometimes the one, sometimes the other, had told me as they bent lovingly over me night after night, what that bell said as it tolled. Many good words has that bell spoken to me through their translations. No wrong thing did I do through the day which that voice from all I knew of heaven and the great Father there did not tell me kindly about ere I sank to sleep, speaking the words so plainly that I knew that the power that moved it had seen all and was not angry, never angry, never, but so very, *very* sorry.

We were rowed over in a small boat to the Edinburgh steamer in the Firth of Forth. As I was about to be taken from the small boat to the steamer, I rushed to Uncle Lauder and clung round his neck, crying out: "I cannot leave you! I cannot leave you!" I was torn from him by a kind sailor who lifted me up on the deck of the steamer. Upon my return visit to Dunfermline this dear old fellow, when he came to see me, told me it was the saddest parting he had ever witnessed.

We sailed from the Broomielaw of Glasgow in the 800-ton sailing ship Wiscasset. During the seven weeks of the voyage, I came to know the sailors quite well, learned the names of the ropes, and was able to direct the passengers to answer the call of the boatswain, for the ship being undermanned, the aid of the passengers was urgently required. In consequence I was invited by the sailors to participate on Sundays, in the one delicacy of the sailors' mess, plum-duff. I left the ship with sincere regret.

The arrival at New York was bewildering. I had been taken to see the Queen at Edinburgh, but that was the extent of my travels before emigrating. Glasgow we had not time to see before we sailed. New York was the first great hive of human industry among the inhabitants of which I had mingled, and the bustle and excitement of it overwhelmed me. The incident of our stay in New York which impressed me most occurred while I was walking through Bowling Green at Castle Garden. I was caught up in the arms of one of the Wiscasset sailors, Robert Barryman, who was decked out in regular Jack-ashore fashion, with blue jacket and white trousers. I thought him the most beautiful man I had ever seen.

He took me to a refreshment stand and ordered a glass of sarsaparilla for me, which I drank with as much relish as if it were the nectar of the gods. To this day nothing that I have ever seen of the kind rivals the image which remains in my mind of the gorgeousness of the highly ornamented brass vessel out of which that nectar came foaming. Often as I have passed the identical spot I see standing there the old woman's sarsaparilla stand, and I marvel what became of the dear old sailor. I have tried to trace him, but in vain, hoping that if found he might be enjoying a ripe old age, and that it might be in my power to add to the pleasure of his declining years. He was my ideal Tom Bowling, and when that fine old song is sung I always see as the "form of manly beauty" my dear old friend Barryman. Alas! ere this he's gone aloft. Well: by his kindness on the voyage he made one boy his devoted friend and admirer.

My father was induced by emigration agents in New York to take the Erie Canal by way of Buffalo and Lake Erie to Cleveland, and thence down the canal to Beaver—a journey which then lasted three weeks, and is made to-day by rail in ten hours. There was no railway communication then with Pittsburgh; nor indeed with any western town. The Erie Railway was under construction and we saw gangs of men at work upon it as we traveled. Nothing comes amiss to youth, and I look back upon my three weeks as a passenger upon the canal-boat with unalloyed pleasure. All that was disagreeable in my experience has long since faded from recollection, excepting the night we were compelled to remain upon the wharf-boat at Beaver waiting for the steamboat to take us up the Ohio to Pittsburgh. This was our first introduction to the mosquito in all its ferocity. My mother suffered so severely that in the morning she could hardly see. We were all frightful sights, but I do not remember that even the stinging misery of that night kept me from sleeping soundly.

Our friends in Pittsburgh had been anxiously waiting to hear from us, and in their warm and affectionate greeting all our troubles were forgotten. We took up our residence with them in Allegheny City. A brother of my Uncle Hogan had built a small weaver's shop at the back end of a lot in Rebecca Street. This had a second story in which there were two rooms, and it was in these (free of rent, for my Aunt Aitken owned them) that my parents began housekeeping. My uncle soon gave up weaving and my father took his place and began making table-cloths, which he had not only to weave, but afterwards, acting as his own merchant, to travel and sell, as no dealers could be found to take them in quantity. He was compelled to market them himself, selling from door to door. The returns were meager in the extreme.

As usual, my mother came to the rescue. There was no keeping her down. In her youth she had learned to bind shoes in her father's business for pin-money, and the skill then acquired was now turned to account for the benefit of the family, and in addition to attending to her household duties—for, of course, we had no servant—this wonderful woman, my mother, earned four dollars a week by binding shoes. Midnight would often find her at work. In the intervals during the day and evening, when household cares would permit, and my young brother sat at her knee threading needles and waxing the thread for her, she recited to him, as she had to me, the gems of Scottish minstrelsy which she seemed to have by heart, or told him tales which failed not to contain a moral.

This is where the children of honest poverty have the most precious of all advantages over those of wealth. The mother, nurse, cook, governess, teacher, saint, all in one; the father, exemplar, guide, counselor, and friend! Thus were my brother and I brought up. What has the child of millionaire or nobleman that counts compared to such a heritage?

My mother was a busy woman, but all her work did not prevent her neighbors from soon recognizing her as a wise and kindly woman whom they could call upon for counsel or help in times of trouble. Many have told me what my mother did for them. So it was in after years wherever we resided; rich and poor came to her with their trials and found good counsel. She towered among her neighbors wherever she went.

CHAPTER III

"ANDY" GOES TO WORK

THE great question now was, what could be found for me to do. I had just completed my thirteenth year, and I fairly panted to get to work that I might help the family to a start in the new land. The prospect of want had become to me a frightful nightmare. My thoughts at this period centered in the determination that we should make and save enough of money to produce three hundred dollars a year—twenty-five dollars monthly, which I figured was the sum required to keep us without being dependent upon others. Every necessary thing was very cheap in those days.

The brother of my Uncle Hogan would often ask what my parents meant to do with me, and one day there occurred the most tragic of all scenes I have ever witnessed. Never can I forget it. He said, with the kindest intentions in the world, to my mother, that I was a likely boy and apt to learn; and he believed that if a basket were fitted out for me with knickknacks to sell, I could peddle them around the wharves and make quite a considerable sum. I never knew what an enraged woman meant till then. My mother was sitting sewing at the moment, but she sprang to her feet with outstretched hands and shook them in his face.

"What! my son a peddler and go among rough men upon the wharves! I would rather throw him into the Allegheny River. Leave me!" she cried, pointing to the door, and Mr. Hogan went.

She stood a tragic queen. The next moment she had broken down, but only for a few moments did tears fall and sobs come. Then she took her two boys in her arms and told us not to mind her foolishness. There were many things in the world for us to do and we could be useful men, honored and respected, if we always did what was right. The suggested occupation was somewhat vagrant in character and not entirely respectable in her eyes. Better death. Yes, mother would have taken her two boys, one under each arm, and perished with them rather than they should mingle with low company in their extreme youth.

As I look back upon the early struggles this can be said: there was not a prouder family in the land. A keen sense of honor, independence, self-respect, pervaded the household. Walter Scott said of Burns that he had the most extraordinary eye he ever saw in a human being. I can say as much for my mother. As Burns has it:

> "Her eye even turned on empty space,
> Beamed keen with honor."

Anything low, mean, deceitful, shifty, coarse, underhand, or gossipy was foreign to that heroic soul. Tom and I could not help growing up respectable characters, having such a mother and such a father, for the father, too, was one of nature's noblemen, beloved by all, a saint.

Soon after this incident my father found it necessary to give up hand-loom weaving and to enter the cotton factory of Mr. Blackstock, an old Scotsman in Allegheny City, where we lived. In this factory he also obtained for me a position as bobbin boy, and my first work was done there at one dollar and twenty cents per week. It was a hard life. In the winter father and I had to rise and breakfast in the darkness, reach the factory before it was daylight, and, with a short interval for lunch, work till after dark. The hours hung heavily upon me and in the work itself I took no pleasure; but the cloud had a silver lining, as it gave me the feeling that I was doing something for my world—our family. I have made millions since, but none of those millions gave me such happiness as my first week's earnings. I was now a helper of the family, a breadwinner, and no longer a total charge upon my parents. Often had I heard my father's beautiful singing of "The Boatie Rows" and often I longed to fulfill the last lines of the verse:

> "When Aaleck, Jock, and Jeanettie,
> *Are up and got their lair,*[1]
> They'll serve to gar the boatie row,
> And lichten a' our care."

I was going to make our tiny craft skim. It should be noted here that Aaleck, Jock, and Jeanettie were first to get their education. Scotland was the first country that required all parents, high or low, to educate their children, and establish the parish public schools.

Soon after this Mr. John Hay, a fellow-Scotch manufacturer of bobbins in Allegheny City, needed a boy, and asked whether I would not go into his service. I went, and received two dollars per week; but at first the work was even more irksome than the factory. I had to run a small steam-engine and to fire the boiler in the cellar of the bobbin factory. It was too much for me. I found myself, night after night, sitting up in bed trying the steam gauges, fearing at one time that the

[1] Education.

steam was too low and that the workers above would complain that they had not power enough, and at another time that the steam was too high and that the boiler might burst.

But all this was a matter of honor to conceal from my parents. They had their own troubles and bore them. I must play the man and bear mine. My hopes were high, and I looked every day for some change to take place. What it was to be I knew not, but that it would come I felt certain if I kept on. Besides, at this date I was not beyond asking myself what Wallace would have done and what a Scotsman ought to do. Of one thing I was sure, he ought never to give up.

One day the chance came. Mr. Hay had to make out some bills. He had no clerk, and was himself a poor penman. He asked me what kind of hand I could write, and gave me some writing to do. The result pleased him, and he found it convenient thereafter to let me make out his bills. I was also good at figures; and he soon found it to be to his interest—and besides, dear old man, I believe he was moved by good feeling toward the white-haired boy, for he had a kind heart and was Scotch and wished to relieve me from the engine—to put me at other things, less objectionable except in one feature.

It now became my duty to bathe the newly made spools in vats of oil. Fortunately there was a room reserved for this purpose and I was alone, but not all the resolution I could muster, nor all the indignation I felt at my own weakness, prevented my stomach from behaving in a most perverse way. I never succeeded in overcoming the nausea produced by the smell of the oil. Even Wallace and Bruce proved impotent here. But if I had to lose breakfast, or dinner, I had all the better appetite for supper, and the allotted work was done. A real disciple of Wallace or Bruce could not give up; he would die first.

My service with Mr. Hay was a distinct advance upon the cotton factory, and I also made the acquaintance of an employer who was very kind to me. Mr. Hay kept his books in single entry, and I was able to handle them for him; but learning that all great firms kept their books in double entry, and after talking over the matter with my companions, John Phipps, Thomas N. Miller, and William Cowley, we all determined to attend night school during the winter and learn the larger system. So the four of us went to a Mr. Williams in Pittsburgh and learned double-entry bookkeeping.

One evening, early in 1850, when I returned home from work, I was told that Mr. David Brooks, manager of the telegraph office, had asked my Uncle Hogan if he knew where a good boy could be found to act as messenger. Mr. Brooks and my uncle were enthusiastic draught-players, and it was over a game of draughts that this important inquiry was made. Upon such trifles do the most momentous consequences hang. A word, a look, an accent, may affect the destiny not only of individuals, but of nations. He is a bold man who calls anything a trifle. Who was it who, being advised to disregard trifles, said he always would if any one could tell him what a trifle was? The young should remember that upon trifles the best gifts of the gods often hang.

My uncle mentioned my name, and said he would see whether I would take the position. I remember so well the family council that was held. Of course I was wild with delight. No bird that ever was confined in a cage longed for freedom more than I. Mother favored, but father was disposed to deny my wish. It would prove too much for me, he said; I was too young and too small. For the two dollars and a half per week offered it was evident that a much larger boy was expected. Late at night I might be required to run out into the country with a telegram, and there would be dangers to encounter. Upon the whole my father said that it was best that I should remain where I was. He subsequently withdrew his objection, so far as to give me leave to try, and I believe he went to Mr. Hay and consulted with him. Mr. Hay thought it would be for my advantage, and although, as he said, it would be an inconvenience to him, still he advised that I should try, and if I failed he was kind enough to say that my old place would be open for me.

This being decided, I was asked to go over the river to Pittsburgh and call on Mr. Brooks. My father wished to go with me, and it was settled that he should accompany me as far as the telegraph office, on the corner of Fourth and Wood Streets. It was a bright, sunshiny morning and this augured well. Father and I walked over from Allegheny to Pittsburgh, a distance of nearly two miles from our house. Arrived at the door I asked father to wait outside. I insisted upon going alone upstairs to the second or operating floor to see the great man and learn my fate. I was led to this, perhaps, because I had by that time begun to consider myself something of an American. At first boys used to call me "Scotchie! Scotchie!" and I answered, "Yes, I'm Scotch and I am proud of the name." But in speech and in address the broad Scotch had been worn off to a slight extent, and I imagined that I could make a smarter showing if alone with Mr. Brooks than if my good old Scotch father were present, perhaps to smile at my airs.

I was dressed in my one white linen shirt, which was usually kept sacred for the Sabbath day, my blue roundabout, and my whole Sunday suit. I had at that time, and for a few weeks after I entered the telegraph service, but one linen suit of summer clothing; and every Saturday night, no matter if that was my night on duty and I did not return till near midnight, my mother washed those clothes and ironed them, and I put them on fresh on Sabbath morning. There was nothing that heroine did not do in the struggle we were making for elbow room in the western world. Father's long factory hours tried his strength, but he, too, fought the good fight like a hero and never failed to encourage me.

The interview was successful. I took care to explain that I did not know Pittsburgh, that perhaps I would not do, would not be strong enough; but all I wanted was a trial. He asked me how soon I could come, and I said that I could stay now if wanted. And, looking back over the circumstance, I think that answer might well be pondered by young men. It is a great mistake not to seize the opportunity. The position was offered to me; something might occur, some other boy might be sent for. Having got myself in I proposed to stay there if I could. Mr. Brooks very kindly called the other boy—for it was an additional messenger that was wanted—and asked him to show me about, and let me go with him and learn the business. I soon found opportunity to run down to the corner of the street and tell my father that it was all right, and to go home and tell mother that I had got the situation.

And that is how in 1850 I got my first real start in

Andrew Carnegie at sixteen with his younger brother Tom.

Carnegie family's first home at
336½ Rebecca Street.
(see p. 15)

Uncle and Aunt Hogan's house in
Rebecca Street
(later 811 Reedsdale Street).
(see p. 53).

Homewood, Penn and Lang Avenue.
(see p. 67).

Andrew Carnegie's early homes in Pittsburgh.

life. From the dark cellar running a steam-engine at two dollars a week, begrimed with coal dirt, without a trace of the elevating influences of life, I was lifted into paradise, yes, heaven, as it seemed to me, with newspapers, pens, pencils, and sunshine about me. There was scarcely a minute in which I could not learn something or find out how much there was to learn and how little I knew. I felt that my foot was upon the ladder and that I was bound to climb.

I had only one fear, and that was that I could not learn quickly enough the addresses of the various business houses to which messages had to be delivered. I therefore began to note the signs of these houses up one side of the street and down the other. At night I exercised my memory by naming in succession the various firms. Before long I could shut my eyes and, beginning at the foot of a business street, call off the names of the firms in proper order along one side to the top of the street, then crossing on the other side go down in regular order to the foot again.

The next step was to know the men themselves, for it gave a messenger a great advantage, and often saved a long journey, if he knew members or employees of firms. He might meet one of these going direct to his office. It was reckoned a great triumph among the boys to deliver a message upon the street. And there was the additional satisfaction to the boy himself, that a great man (and most men are great to messengers), stopped upon the street in this way, seldom failed to note the boy and compliment him.

The Pittsburgh of 1850 was very different from what it has since become. It had not yet recovered from the great fire which destroyed the entire business portion of the city on April 10, 1845. The houses were mainly of wood, a few only were of brick, and not one was fireproof. The entire population in and around Pittsburgh was not over forty thousand. The business portion of the city did not extend as far as Fifth Avenue, which was then a very quiet street, remarkable only for having the theater upon it. Federal Street, Allegheny, consisted of straggling business houses with great open spaces between them, and I remember skating upon ponds in the very heart of the present Fifth Ward. The site of our Union Iron Mills was then, and many years later, a cabbage garden.

General Robinson, to whom I delivered many a telegraph message, was the first white child born west of the Ohio River. I saw the first telegraph line stretched from the east into the city; and, at a later date, I also saw the first locomotive, for the Ohio and Pennsylvania Railroad, brought by canal from Philadelphia and unloaded from a scow in Allegheny City. There was no direct railway communication to the East. Passengers took the canal to the foot of the Allegheny Mountains, over which they were transported to Hollidaysburg, a distance of thirty miles by rail; thence by canal again to Columbia, and then eighty-one miles by rail to Philadelphia—a journey which occupied three days.

The great event of the day in Pittsburgh at that time was the arrival and departure of the steam packet to and from Cincinnati, for daily communication had been established. The business of the city was largely that of forwarding merchandise East and West, for it was the great transfer station from river to canal. A rolling mill had begun to roll iron; but not a ton of pig metal was made, and not a ton of steel for many a year thereafter. The pig iron manufacture at first was a total failure because of the lack of proper fuel, although the most valuable deposit of coking coal in the world lay within a few miles, as much undreamt of for coke to smelt iron-stone as the stores of natural gas which had for ages lain untouched under the city.

CHAPTER IV

WHY CARNEGIE FOUNDED LIBRARIES

MY life as a telegraph messenger was in every respect a happy one, and it was while in this position that I laid the foundation of my closest friendships. The senior message boy being promoted, a new boy was needed, and he came in the person of David McCargo, afterwards the well-known superintendent of the Allegheny Valley Railway. He was made my companion and we had to deliver all the messages from the Eastern line, while two other boys delivered the messages from the West. The Eastern and Western Telegraph Companies were then separate, although occupying the same building. "Davy" and I became firm friends at once, one great bond being that he was Scotch; for, although "Davy" was born in America, his father was quite as much a Scotsman, even in speech, as my own father.

A short time after "Davy's" appointment a third boy was required, and this time I was asked if I could find a suitable one. This I had no difficulty in doing in my chum, Robert Pitcairn, later on my successor as superintendent and general agent at Pittsburgh of the Pennsylvania Railroad. Robert, like myself, was not only Scotch, but Scotch-born, so that "Davy," "Bob," and "Andy" became the three Scotch boys who delivered all the messages of the Eastern Telegraph Line in Pittsburgh, for the then magnificent salary of two and a half dollars per week. It was the duty of the boys to sweep the office each morning, and this we did in turn, so it will be seen that we all began at the bottom. It is not the rich man's son that the young struggler for advancement has to fear in the race of life, nor his nephew, nor his cousin. Let him look out for the "dark horse" in the boy who begins by sweeping out the office.

A messenger boy in those days had many pleasures. There were wholesale fruit stores, where a pocketful of apples was sometimes to be had for the prompt delivery of a message; bakers' and confectioners' shops, where sweet cakes were sometimes given to him. He met with very kind men, to whom he looked up with respect; they spoke a pleasant word and complimented him on his promptness, perhaps asked him to deliver a message on the way back to the office. I do not know a situation in which a boy is more apt to attract attention, which is all a really clever boy requires in order to rise. Wise men are always looking out for clever boys.

One great excitement of this life was the extra charge of ten cents which we were permitted to collect for messages delivered beyond a certain limit. These "dime messages," as might be expected, were anxiously watched, and quarrels arose among us as to the right of delivery. In some cases it was alleged boys had now and then taken a dime message out of turn. This was the only cause of serious trouble among us. By way of settlement I proposed that we should "pool" these messages and divide the cash equally at the end of each week. I was appointed treasurer. Peace and good-humor reigned ever afterwards. This pooling of extra earnings was my first essay in financial organization.

The boys considered that they had a perfect right to spend these dividends, and the adjoining confectioner's shop had running accounts with most of them. The accounts were sometimes greatly overdrawn. The treasurer had accordingly to notify the confectioner, which he did in due form, that he would not be responsible for any debts contracted by the too hungry and greedy boys. Robert Pitcairn was the worst offender of all, apparently having not only one sweet tooth, but all his teeth of that character. He explained to me confidentially one day, when I scolded him, that he had live things in his stomach that gnawed his insides until fed upon sweets.

With all their pleasures the messenger boys were hard worked. Every other evening they were required to be on duty until the office closed, and on those nights it was seldom that I reached home before eleven o'clock. On the alternating nights we were relieved at six. This did not leave much time for self-improvement, nor did the wants of the family leave any money to spend on books. There came, however, like a blessing from above, a means by which the treasures of literature were unfolded to me.

Colonel James Anderson—I bless his name as I write—announced that he would open his library of four hundred volumes to boys, so that any young man could take out, each Saturday afternoon, a book which could be exchanged for another on the succeeding Saturday. Colonel Anderson's books were first opened to "working boys," and the question arose whether messenger boys, clerks, and others, who did not work with their hands, were entitled to books. My first communication to the press was a note, written to the *Pittsburgh Dispatch*, urging that we should not be excluded; that although we did not now work with our hands, some of us had done so, and that we were really working boys. Dear Colonel Anderson promptly enlarged the classification. So my first appearance as a public writer was a success.

My dear friend, Tom Miller, one of the inner circle, lived near Colonel Anderson and introduced me to him, and in this way the windows were opened in the walls of my dungeon through which the light of knowledge streamed in. Every day's toil and even the long hours of night service were lightened by the book which I carried about with me and read in the intervals that could be snatched from duty. And the future was made bright by the thought that when Saturday came a new volume could be obtained. In this way I became familiar with Macaulay's essays and his history, and with Bancroft's *History of the United States*, which I studied with more care than any other book I had then read. Lamb's essays were my special delight, but I had at this time no knowledge of the great master of all, Shakespeare, beyond the selected pieces in the school books. My taste for him I acquired a little later at the old Pittsburgh Theater.

John Phipps, James R. Wilson, Thomas N. Miller, William Cowley—members of our circle—shared with me the invaluable privilege of the use of Colonel Anderson's library. Books which it would have been impossible for me to obtain elsewhere were, by his wise generosity, placed within my reach; and to him I owe a taste for literature which I would not exchange for all the millions that were ever amassed by man. Nothing contributed so much to keep my companions and myself clear of low fellowship and bad habits as the beneficence of the good Colonel. Later, when fortune smiled upon me, one of my first duties was the erection of a monument to my benefactor. It stands in front of the Hall and Library in Diamond Square, which I presented to Allegheny, and bears this inscription:

> To Colonel James Anderson, Founder of Free Libraries in West Pennsylvania. He opened his Library to working boys and upon Saturday afternoons acted as librarian, thus dedicating not only his books but himself to the noble work. This monument is erected in grateful remembrance by Andrew Carnegie, one of the "working boys" to whom were thus opened the precious treasures of knowledge and imagination through which youth may ascend.

This is but a slight tribute and gives only a faint idea of the depth of gratitude which I feel for what he did for me and my companions. It was from my own early experience that I decided there was no use to which money could be applied so productive of good to boys and girls who have good within them and ability and ambition to develop it, as the founding of a public library in a community which is willing to support it as a municipal institution. I am sure that the future of those libraries I have been privileged to found will prove the correctness of this opinion. For if one boy in each library district, by having access to one of these libraries, is half as much benefited as I was by having access to Colonel Anderson's four hundred well-worn volumes, I shall consider they have not been established in vain.

"As the twig is bent the tree's inclined." The treasures of the world which books contain were opened to me at the right moment. The fundamental advantage of a library is that it gives nothing for nothing. Youths must acquire knowledge themselves. There is no escape from this. It gave me great satisfaction to discover, many years later, that my father was one of the five weavers in Dunfermline who gathered together the few books they had and formed the first circulating library in that town.

The history of that library is interesting. It grew, and was removed no less than seven times from place to place, the first move being made by the founders, who carried the books in their aprons and two coal scuttles from the hand-loom shop to the second resting-place. That my father was one of the founders of the first library in his native town, and that I have been fortunate enough to be the founder of the last one, is certainly to me one of the most interesting incidents of my life. I have said often, in public speeches, that I had never heard of a lineage for which I would exchange that of a library-founding weaver. I followed my father in library founding unknowingly—I am tempted almost to say providentially—and it has been a source of intense satisfaction to me. Such a father as mine was a guide to be followed—one of the sweetest, purest, and kindest natures I have ever known.

I have stated that it was the theater which first stimulated my love for Shakespeare. In my messenger days the old Pittsburgh Theater was in its glory under the charge of Mr. Foster. His telegraphic business was done free, and the telegraph operators were given free admission to the theater in return. This privilege extended in some degree also to the messengers, who, I fear, sometimes withheld telegrams that arrived for him in the late afternoon until they could be presented at the door of the theater in the evening, with the timid request that the messenger might be allowed to slip upstairs to the second tier—a request which was always granted. The boys exchanged duties to give each the coveted entrance in turn.

In this way I became acquainted with the world that lay behind the green curtain. The plays, generally, were of the spectacular order; without much literary merit, but well calculated to dazzle the eye of a youth of fifteen. Not only had I never seen anything so grand, but I had never seen anything of the kind. I had never been in a theater, or even a concert room, or seen any form of public amusement. It was much the same with "Davy" McCargo, "Harry" Oliver, and "Bob" Pitcairn. We all fell under the fascination of the footlights, and every opportunity to attend the theater was eagerly embraced.

A change in my tastes came when "Gust" Adams,[1] one of the most celebrated tragedians of the day, began to play in Pittsburgh a round of Shakespearean characters. Thenceforth there was nothing for me but Shakespeare. I seemed to be able to memorize him almost without effort. Never before had I realized what magic lay in words. The rhythm and the melody all seemed to find a resting-place in me, to melt into a solid mass which lay ready to come at call. It was a new language and its appreciation I certainly owe to dramatic representation, for, until I saw "Macbeth" played, my interest in Shakespeare was not aroused. I had not read the plays.

At a much later date, Wagner was revealed to me in *Lohengrin*. I had heard, at the Academy of Music in New York, little or nothing by him when the overture to *Lohengrin* thrilled me as a new revelation. Here was a genius, indeed, differing from all before, a new ladder upon which to climb upward—like Shakespeare, a new friend.

I may speak here of another matter which belongs

[1] Edwin Adams.

to this same period. A few persons in Allegheny—probably not above a hundred in all—had formed themselves into a Swedenborgian Society, in which our American relatives were prominent. My father attended that church after leaving the Presbyterian, and, of course, I was taken there.

It was in connection with the Swedenborgian Society that a taste for music was first aroused in me. As an appendix to the hymn-book of the society there were short selections from the oratorios. I fastened instinctively upon these, and although denied much of a voice, yet credited with "expression," I was a constant attendant upon choir practice. The leader, I have reason to believe, often pardoned the discords I produced in the choir because of my enthusiasm in the cause. When, at a later date, I became acquainted with the oratorios in full, it was a pleasure to find that several of those considered in musical circles as the gems of Handel's musical compositions were the ones that I as an ignorant boy had chosen as favorites. So the beginning of my musical education dates from the small choir of the Swedenborgian Society of Pittsburgh.

I must not, however, forget that a very good foundation was laid for my love of sweet sounds in the unsurpassed minstrelsy of my native land as sung by my father. There was scarcely an old Scottish song with which I was not made familiar, both words and tune. Folk-songs are the best possible foundation for sure progress to the heights of Beethoven and Wagner. My father being one of the sweetest and most pathetic singers I ever heard, I probably inherited his love of music and of song, though not given his voice.

CHAPTER V

IN THE TELEGRAPH OFFICE

I HAD served as messenger about a year, when Colonel John P. Glass, the manager of the downstairs office, who came in contact with the public, began selecting me occasionally to watch the office for a few minutes during his absence. As Mr. Glass was a highly popular man, and had political aspirations, these periods of absence became longer and more frequent, so that I soon became an adept in his branch of the work. I received messages from the public and saw that those that came from the operating-room were properly assigned to the boys for prompt delivery.

This was a trying position for a boy to fill, and at that time I was not popular with the other boys, who resented my exemption from part of my legitimate work. I was also taxed with being penurious in my habits—mean, as the boys had it. I did not spend my extra dimes, but they knew not the reason. Every penny that I could save I knew was needed at home. My parents were wise and nothing was withheld from me. I knew every week the receipts of each of the three who were working—my father, my mother, and myself. I also knew all the expenditures. We consulted upon the additions that could be made to our scanty stock of furniture and clothing and every new small article obtained was a source of joy. There never was a family more united.

Day by day, as mother could spare a silver half-dollar, it was carefully placed in a stocking and hid until two hundred were gathered, when I obtained a draft to repay the twenty pounds so generously lent to us by her friend Mrs. Henderson. That was a day we celebrated. The Carnegie family was free from debt. Oh, the happiness of that day! The debt was, indeed, discharged, but the debt of gratitude remains that never can be paid.

The incident in my messenger life which at once lifted me to the seventh heaven, occurred one Saturday evening when Colonel Glass was paying the boys their month's wages. We stood in a row before the counter, and Mr. Glass paid each one in turn. I was at the head and reached out my hand for the first eleven and a quarter dollars as they were pushed out by Mr. Glass. To my surprise he pushed them past me and paid the next boy. I thought it was a mistake, for I had heretofore been paid first, but it followed in turn with each of the other boys. My heart began to sink within me. Disgrace seemed coming. What had I done or not done? I was about to be told that there was no more work for me. I was to disgrace the family. That was the keenest pang of all. When all had been paid and the boys were gone, Mr. Glass took me behind the counter and said that I was worth more than the other boys, and he had resolved to pay me thirteen and a half dollars a month.

My head swam; I doubted whether I had heard him correctly. He counted out the money. I don't know whether I thanked him; I don't believe I did. I took it and made one bound for the door and scarcely stopped until I got home. I remember distinctly running or rather bounding from end to end of the bridge across the Allegheny River—inside on the wagon track because the footwalk was too narrow. It was Saturday night. I handed over to mother, who was the treasurer of the family, the eleven dollars and a quarter and said nothing about the remaining two dollars and a quarter in my pocket—worth more to me then than all the millions I have made since.

Tom, a little boy of nine, and myself slept in the attic together, and after we were safely in bed I whispered the secret to my dear little brother. Even at his early age he knew what it meant, and we talked over the future. It was then, for the first time, I sketched to him how we would go into business together; that the firm of "Carnegie Brothers" would be a great one, and that father and mother should yet ride in their carriage. At the time that seemed to us to embrace everything known as wealth and most of what was worth striving for. The old Scotchwoman, whose daughter married a merchant in London, being asked by her son-in-law to come to London and live near them, promising she should "ride in her carriage," replied:

"What good could it do me to ride in a carriage gin I could na be seen by the folk in Strathbogie?" Father and mother would not only be seen in Pittsburgh, but should visit Dunfermline, their old home, in style.

On Sunday morning with father, mother, and Tom at breakfast, I produced the extra two dollars and a quarter. The surprise was great and it took some moments for them to grasp the situation, but it soon dawned upon them. Then father's glance of loving pride, and mother's blazing eye soon wet with tears, told their feeling. It was their boy's first triumph and proof positive that he was worthy of promotion. No subsequent success, or recognition of any kind, ever thrilled me as this did. I cannot even imagine one that could. Here was heaven upon earth. My whole world was moved to tears of joy.

Having to sweep out the operating-room in the mornings, the boys had an opportunity of practicing upon the telegraph instruments before the operators arrived. This was a new chance. I soon began to play with the key and to talk with the boys who were at the other stations who had like purposes to my own. Whenever one learns to do anything he has never to wait long for an opportunity of putting his knowledge to use.

One morning I heard the Pittsburgh call given with vigor. It seemed to me I could divine that some one wished greatly to communicate. I ventured to answer, and let the slip run. It was Philadelphia that wanted to send "a death message" to Pittsburgh immediately. Could I take it? I replied that I would try if they would send slowly. I succeeded in getting the message and ran out with it. I waited anxiously for Mr. Brooks to come in, and told him what I had dared to do. Fortunately, he appreciated it and complimented me, instead of scolding me for my temerity; yet dismissing me with the admonition to be very careful and not to make mistakes. It was not long before I was called sometimes to watch the instrument, while the operator wished to be absent, and in this way I learned the art of telegraphy.

We were blessed at this time with a rather indolent operator, who was only too glad to have me do his work. It was then the practice for us to receive the messages on a running slip of paper, from which the operator read to a copyist, but rumours had reached us that a man in the West had learned to read by sound and could really take a message by ear. This led me to practice the new method. One of the operators in the office became expert at it, and encouraged me by his success. I was surprised at the ease with which I learned the new language. One day, desiring to take a message in the absence of the operator, the old gentleman who acted as copyist resented my presumption and refused to "copy" for a messenger boy. I shut off the paper slip, took pencil and paper and began taking the message by ear. I shall never forget his surprise. He ordered me to give him back his pencil and pad, and after that there was never any difficulty between dear old Courtney Hughes and myself. He was my devoted friend and copyist.

Soon after this incident, the operator at Greensburg, thirty miles from Pittsburgh, wishing to be absent for two weeks, asked Mr. Brooks if he could not send some one to take his place. Mr. Brooks called me and asked whether I thought I could do the work. I replied at once in the affirmative.

"Well," he said, "we will send you out there for a trial."

I went out in the mail stage and had a most delightful trip. It was my first excursion, and my first glimpse of the country. The hotel at Greensburg was the first public house in which I had ever taken a meal. I thought the food wonderfully fine.

This was in 1852. Deep cuts and embankments near Greensburg were then being made for the Pennsylvania Railroad, and I often walked out in the early morning to see the work going forward, little dreaming that I was so soon to enter the service of that great corporation. This was the first responsible position I had occupied in the telegraph service, and I was so anxious to be at hand in case I should be needed, that one night very late I sat in the office during a storm, not wishing to cut off the connection. I ventured too near the key and for my boldness was knocked off my stool. A flash of lightning very nearly ended my career. After that I was noted in the office for caution during lightning storms. I succeeded in doing the small business at Greensburg to the satisfaction of my superiors, and returned to Pittsburgh surrounded with something like a halo, so far as the other boys were concerned. Promotion soon came. A new operator was wanted and Mr. Brooks telegraphed to my afterward dear friend James D. Reid, then general superintendent of the line, another fine specimen of the Scotsman, and took upon himself to recommend me as an assistant operator. The telegram from Louisville in reply stated that Mr. Reid highly approved of promoting "Andy," provided Mr. Brooks considered him competent. The result was that I began as a telegraph operator at the tremendous salary of twenty-five dollars per month, which I thought a fortune. I was then in my seventeenth year and had served my apprenticeship. I was now performing a man's part, no longer a boy's—earning a dollar every working day.

The operating-room of a telegraph office is an excellent school for a young man. He there has to do with pencil and paper, with composition and invention. And there my slight knowledge of British and European affairs soon stood me in good stead. Knowledge is sure to prove useful in one way or another. It always tells. The foreign news was then received by wire from Cape Race, and the taking of successive "steamer news" was one of the most notable of our duties. I liked this better than any other branch of the work, and it was soon tacitly assigned to me.

The lines in those days worked poorly, and during

a storm much had to be guessed at. My guessing powers were said to be phenomenal, and it was my favorite diversion to fill up gaps instead of interrupting the sender and spending minutes over a lost word or two. This was not a dangerous practice in regard to foreign news, for if any undue liberties were taken by the bold operator, they were not of a character likely to bring him into serious trouble. My knowledge of foreign affairs became somewhat extensive, especially regarding the affairs of Britain, and my guesses were quite safe, if I got the first letter or two right.

The Pittsburgh newspapers had each been in the habit of sending a reporter to the office to transcribe the press dispatches. Later on one man was appointed for all the papers and he suggested that multiple copies could readily be made of the news as received, and it was arranged that I should make five copies of all press dispatches for him as extra work for which he was to pay me a dollar per week. This, my first work for the press, yielded very modest remuneration, to be sure; but it made my salary thirty dollars per month, and every dollar counted in those days. The family was gradually gaining ground; already future millionaire-dom seemed dawning.

Another step which exercised a decided influence over me was joining the "Webster Literary Society" along with my companions, the trusty five already named. We formed a select circle and stuck closely together. This was quite an advantage for all of us. We had before this formed a small debating club which met in Mr. Phipps's father's room in which his few journeymen shoemakers worked during the day. Tom Miller recently alleged that I once spoke nearly an hour and a half upon the question, "Should the judiciary be elected by the people?" but we must mercifully assume his memory to be at fault. The "Webster" was then the foremost club in the city and proud were we to be thought fit for membership. We had merely been preparing ourselves in the cobbler's room.

I know of no better mode of benefiting a youth than joining such a club as this. Much of my reading became such as had a bearing on forthcoming debates and that gave clearness and fixity to my ideas. The self-possession I afterwards came to have before an audience may very safely be attributed to the experience of the "Webster Society." My two rules for speaking then (and now) were: Make yourself perfectly at home before your audience, and simply talk *to* them, not *at* them. Do not try to be somebody else; be your own self and *talk*, never "orate" until you can't help it.

I finally became an operator by sound, discarding printing entirely. The accomplishment was then so rare that people visited the office to be satisfied of the extraordinary feat. This brought me into such notice that when a great flood destroyed all telegraph communication between Steubenville and Wheeling, a distance of twenty-five miles, I was sent to the former town to receive the entire business then passing between the East and the West, and to send every hour or two the dispatches in small boats down the river to Wheeling. In exchange every returning boat brought rolls of dispatches which I wired East, and in this way for more than a week the entire telegraphic communcation between the East and the West *via* Pittsburgh was maintained.

While at Steubenville I learned that my father was going to Wheeling and Cincinnati to sell the tablecloths he had woven. I waited for the boat, which did not arrive till late in the evening, and went down to meet him. I remember how deeply affected I was on finding that instead of taking a cabin passage, he had resolved not to pay the price, but to go down the river as a deck passenger. I was indignant that one of so fine a nature should be compelled to travel thus. But there was comfort in saying:

"Well, father, it will not be long before mother and you shall ride in your carriage."

My father was usually shy, reserved, and keenly sensitive, very saving of praise (a Scotch trait) lest his sons might be too greatly uplifted; but when touched he lost his self-control. He was so upon this occasion, and grasped my hand with a look which I often see and can never forget. He murmured slowly:

"Andra, I am proud of you."

The voice trembled and he seemed ashamed of himself for saying so much. The tear had to be wiped from his eye, I fondly noticed, as he bade me good-night and told me to run back to my office. Those words rang in my ear and warmed my heart for years and years. We understood each other. My father was one of the most lovable of men, beloved of his companions, deeply religious, not much of a man of the world, but a man all over for heaven. He was kindness itself, although reserved. Alas! he passed away soon after returning from this Western tour just as we were becoming able to give him a life of leisure and comfort.

After my return to Pittsburgh it was not long before I made the acquaintance of an extraordinary man, Thomas A. Scott, one to whom the term "genius" in his department may safely be applied. He had come to Pittsburgh as superintendent of that division of the Pennsylvania Railroad. Frequent telegraphic communication was necessary between him and his superior, Mr. Lombaert, general superintendent at Altoona. This brought him to the telegraph office at nights, and upon several occasions I happened to be the operator. One day I was surprised by one of his assistants with whom I was acquainted, telling me that Mr. Scott had asked him whether he thought that I could be obtained as his clerk and telegraph operator, to which this young man told me he had replied:

"That is impossible. He is now an operator."

But when I heard this I said at once:

"Not so fast. He can have me. I want to get out of a mere office life. Please go and tell him so."

The result was I was engaged February 1, 1853, at a salary of thirty-five dollars a month as Mr. Scott's clerk and operator. A raise in wages from twenty-five to thirty-five dollars per month was the greatest I had ever known. The public telegraph line was temporarily put into Mr. Scott's office at the outer depot and the Pennsylvania Railroad Company was given permission to use the wire at seasons when such use would not interfere with the general public business, until their own line, then being built, was completed.

CHAPTER VI

"ANDY" AND THE PENNSYLVANIA RAILROAD

FROM the operating-room of the telegraph office I had now stepped into the open world, and the change at first was far from agreeable. I had just reached my eighteenth birthday, and I do not see how it could be possible for any boy to arrive at that age much freer from a knowledge of anything but what was pure and good. I do not believe I had ever spoken a bad word in my life and seldom heard one. I knew nothing of the base and the vile. Fortunately I had always been brought in contact with good people.

I was now plunged at once into the company of coarse men, for the office was temporarily only a portion of the shops and the headquarters for the freight conductors, brakemen, and firemen. All of them had access to the same room with Superintendent Scott and myself, and they availed themselves of it. This was a different world, indeed, from that to which I had been accustomed. But there were still the sweet and pure surroundings of home, where nothing coarse or wicked ever entered, and besides, there was the world in which I dwelt with my companions, all of them refined young men, striving to improve themselves and become respected citizens.

I do not wish to suggest that the men of whom I have spoken were really degraded or bad characters. Coarse talk, chewing and smoking tobacco were more prevalent then than to-day and meant less than in this age. Railroading was new, and many rough characters were attracted to it from the river service. But many of the men were fine young fellows who have lived to be highly respectable citizens and to occupy responsible positions. And I must say that one and all of them were most kind to me.

I was soon sent by Mr. Scott to Altoona to get the monthly pay-rolls and checks. The railroad line was not completed over the Allegheny Mountains at that time, and I had to pass over the inclined planes which made the journey a remarkable one to me. Altoona was then composed of a few houses built by the company. The shops were under construction and there was nothing of the large city which now occupies the site. It was there I saw for the first time the great man in our railroad field—Mr. Lombaert, general superintendent. His secretary at that time was my friend, Robert Pitcairn, for whom I had obtained a situation on the railroad, so that "Davy," "Bob," and "Andy" were still together in the same service. We had all left the telegraph company for the Pennsylvania Railroad Company.

Mr. Lombaert was very different from Mr. Scott; he was not sociable, but rather stern and unbending. Judge then of Robert's surprise, and my own, when, after saying a few words to me, Mr. Lombaert added: "You must come down and take tea with us to-night." I stammered out something of acceptance and awaited the appointed hour with great trepidation. Up to this time I considered that invitation the greatest honor I had received. Mrs. Lombaert was exceedingly kind, and Mr. Lombaert's introduction of me to her was: "This is Mr. Scott's 'Andy.'" I was very proud indeed of being recognized as belonging to Mr. Scott.

An incident happened on this trip which might have blasted my career for a time. I started next morning for Pittsburgh with the pay-rolls and checks, as I thought, securely placed under my waistcoat, as it was too large a package for my pockets. I was a very enthusiastic railroader at that time and preferred riding upon the engine. I got upon the engine that took me to Hollidaysburg where the State railroad over the mountain was joined up. It was a very rough ride, indeed, and at one place, uneasily feeling for the pay-roll package, I was horrified to find that the jolting of the train had shaken it out. I had lost it!

There was no use in disguising the fact that such a failure would ruin me. To have been sent for the pay-rolls and checks and to lose the package, which I should have "grasped as my honor," was a dreadful showing. I called the engineer and told him it must have been shaken out within the last few miles. Would he reverse his engine and run back for it? Kind soul, he did so. I watched the line, and on the very banks of a large stream, within a few feet of the water, I saw that package lying. I could scarcely believe my eyes. I ran down and grasped it. It was all right. Need I add that it never passed out of my firm grasp again until it was safe in Pittsburgh? The engineer and fireman were the only persons who knew of my carelessness, and I had their assurance that it would not be told.

It was long after the event that I ventured to tell the story. Suppose that package had fallen just a few feet farther away and been swept down by the stream, how many years of faithful service would it have required upon my part to wipe out the effect of that one piece of carelessness! I could no longer have enjoyed the confidence of those whose confidence was essential to success had fortune not favored me. I have never since believed in being too hard on a young man, even if he does commit a dreadful mistake or two; and I have always tried in judging such to remember the difference it would have made in my own career but for an accident which restored to me that lost package at the edge of the stream a few miles from Hollidaysburg. I could go straight to the very spot to-day, and often as I passed over that line afterwards I never failed to see that light-brown package lying upon the bank. It seemed to be calling:

"All right, my boy! the good gods were with you, but don't do it again!"

It was not long after this that the railroad company constructed its own telegraph line. We had to supply it with operators. Most of these were taught in our offices at Pittsburgh. The telegraph business continued to increase with startling rapidity. We could scarcely provide facilities fast enough. New telegraph offices were required. My fellow messenger-boy, "Davy" McCargo, I appointed superintendent of the telegraph department March 11, 1859. I have been told that "Davy" and myself are entitled to the credit of being the first to employ young women as telegraph operators in the United States upon railroads, or perhaps in any branch. At all events, we placed girls in various offices as pupils, taught and then put them in charge of offices as occasion required.

Mr. Scott was one of the most delightful superiors that anybody could have and I soon became warmly attached to him. He was my great man and all the hero worship that is inherent in youth I showered upon him. I soon began placing him in imagination in the presidency of the great Pennsylvania Railroad—a position which he afterwards attained. Under him I gradually performed duties not strictly belonging to my department and I can attribute my decided advancement in the service to one well-remembered incident.

The railway was a single line. Telegraph orders to trains often became necessary, although it was not then a regular practice to run trains by telegraph. No one but the superintendent himself was permitted to give a train order on any part of the Pennsylvania system, or indeed of any other system, I believe, at that time. It was then a dangerous experiment to give telegraphic orders, for the whole system of railway management was still in its infancy, and men had not yet been trained for it. It was necessary for Mr. Scott to go out night after night to break-downs or wrecks to superintend the clearing of the line. He was necessarily absent from the office on many mornings.

One morning I reached the office and found that a serious accident on the Eastern Division had delayed the express passenger train westward, and that the passenger train eastward was proceeding with a flagman in advance at every curve. The freight trains in both directions were all standing still upon the sidings. Mr. Scott was not to be found. Finally I could not resist the temptation to plunge in, take the responsibility, give "train orders," and set matters going. "Death or Westminster Abbey," flashed across my mind. I knew it was dismissal, disgrace, perhaps criminal punishment for me if I erred. On the other hand, I could bring in the wearied freight-train men who had lain out all night. I could set everything in motion. I knew I could. I had often done it in wiring

Mr. Scott's orders. I knew just what to do, and so I began. I gave the orders in his name, started every train, sat at the instrument watching every tick, carried the trains along from station to station, took extra precautions, and had everything running smoothly when Mr. Scott at last reached the office. He had heard of the delays. His first words were:

"Well! How are matters?"

He came to my side quickly, grasped his pencil and began to write his orders. I had then to speak, and timidly said:

"Mr. Scott, I could not find you anywhere and I gave these orders in your name early this morning."

"Are they going all right? Where is the Eastern Express?"

I showed him the messages and gave him the position of every train on the line—freights, ballast trains, everything—showed him the answers of the various conductors, the latest reports at the stations where the various trains had passed. All was right. He looked in my face for a second. I scarcely dared look in his. I did not know what was going to happen. He did not say one word, but again looked carefully over all that had taken place. Still he said nothing. After a little he moved away from my desk to his own, and that was the end of it. He was afraid to approve what I had done, yet he had not censured me. If it came out all right, it was all right; if it came out all wrong, the responsibility was mine. So it stood, but I noticed that he came in very regularly and in good time for some mornings after that.

Of course I never spoke to any one about it. None of the trainmen knew that Mr. Scott had not personally given the orders. I had almost made up my mind that if the like occurred again, I would not repeat my proceeding of that morning unless I was authorized to do so. I was feeling rather distressed about what I had done until I heard from Mr. Franciscus, who was then in charge of the freighting department at Pittsburgh, that Mr. Scott, the evening after the memorable morning, had said to him:

"Do you know what that little white-haired Scotchman of mine did?"

"No."

"Ran every train on the division in my name without the slightest authority."

"And did he do it all right?" asked Franciscus.

"Oh, yes, all right."

This satisfied me. Of course I had my cue for the next occasion, and went boldly in. From that date it was very seldom that Mr. Scott gave a train order.

Some time after this Mr. Scott wished to travel for a week or two and asked authority from Mr. Lombaert to leave me in charge of the division. Pretty bold man he was, for I was then not very far out of my teens. It was granted. Here was the coveted opportunity of my life. With the exception of one accident caused by the inexcusable negligence of a ballast-train crew, everything went well in his absence. But that this accident should occur was gall and wormwood to me. Determined to fulfill all the duties of the station I held a court-martial, examined those concerned, dismissed peremptorily the chief offender, and suspended two others for their share in the catastrophe. Mr. Scott after his return of course was advised of the accident, and proposed to investigate and deal with the matter. I felt I had gone too far, but having taken the step, I informed him that all that had been settled. I had investigated the matter and punished the guilty. Some of these appealed to Mr. Scott for a reopening of the case, but this I never could have agreed to, had it been pressed. More by look I think than by word Mr. Scott understood my feelings upon this delicate point, and acquiesced.

It is probable he was afraid I had been too severe and very likely he was correct. Some years after this, when I, myself, was superintendent of the division I always had a soft spot in my heart for the men then suspended for a time. I had felt qualms of conscience about my action in this, my first court. A new judge is very apt to stand so straight as really to lean a little backward. Only experience teaches the supreme force of gentleness. Light but certain punishment, when necessary, is most effective. Severe punishments are not needed and a judicious pardon, for the first offense at least, is often best of all.

During these years of which I have been writing, the family fortunes had been steadily improving. My thirty-five dollars a month had grown to forty, an unsolicited advance having been made by Mr. Scott. It was part of my duty to pay the men every month. We used checks upon the bank and I drew my salary invariably in two twenty-dollar gold pieces. They seemed to me the prettiest works of art in the world. It was decided in family council that we could venture to buy the lot and the two small frame houses upon it, in one of which we had lived, and the other, a four-roomed house, which till then had been occupied by my Uncle and Aunt Hogan, who had removed elsewhere. It was through the aid of my dear Aunt Aitken that we had been placed in the small house above the weaver's shop, and it was now our turn to be able to ask her to return to the house that formerly had been her own. In the same way after we had occupied the four-roomed house, Uncle Hogan having passed away, we were able to restore Aunt Hogan to her old home when we removed to Altoona. One hundred dollars cash was paid upon purchase, and the total price, as I remember, was seven hundred dollars. The struggle then was to make up the semi-annual payments of interest and as great an amount of the principal as we could save. It was not long before the debt was cleared off and we were property-holders, but before that was accomplished, the first sad break occurred in our family, in my father's death, October 2, 1855. Fortunately for the three remaining members life's duties were pressing. Sorrow and duty contended and we had to work. The expenses connected with his illness had to be saved and paid and we had not up to this time much store in reserve.

And here comes in one of the sweet incidents of our early life in America. The principal member of our small Swedenborgian Society was Mr. David McCandless. He had taken some notice of my father and mother, but beyond a few passing words at church on Sundays, I do not remember that they had ever been brought in close contact. He knew Aunt Aitken well, however, and now sent for her to say that if my mother required any money assistance at this sad period he would be very pleased to advance whatever was necessary. He had heard much of my heroic mother and that was sufficient.

One gets so many kind offers of assistance when assistance is no longer necessary, or when one is in a position which would probably enable him to repay a favor, that it is delightful to record an act of pure and disinterested benevolence. Here was a poor Scottish woman bereft of her husband, with her eldest son just getting a start and a second in his early teens, whose misfortunes appealed to this man, and who in the most delicate manner sought to mitigate them. Although my mother was able to decline the proffered aid, it is needless to say that Mr. McCandless obtained a place in our hearts sacred to himself. I am a firm believer in the doctrine that people deserving necessary assistance at critical periods in their career usually receive it. There are many splendid natures in the world—men and women who are not only willing, but anxious to stretch forth a helping hand to those they know to be worthy. As a rule, those who show willingness to help themselves need not fear about obtaining the help of others.

Father's death threw upon me the management of affairs to a greater extent than ever. Mother kept on the binding of shoes; Tom went steadily to the public school; and I continued with Mr. Scott in the service of the railroad company. Just at this time Fortunatus knocked at our door. Mr. Scott asked me if I had five hundred dollars. If so, he said he wished to make an investment for me. Five hundred cents was much nearer my capital. I certainly had not fifty dollars saved for investment, but I was not going to miss the chance of becoming financially connected with my leader and great men. So I said boldly I thought I could manage that sum. He then told me that there were ten shares of Adams Express stock that he could buy. Of course this was reported to the head of the family that evening, and she was not long in suggesting what might be done. When did she ever fail? We had then paid five hundred dollars upon the house, and in some way she thought this might be pledged as security for a loan.

My mother took the steamer the next morning for East Liverpool, arriving at night, and through her brother there the money was secured. He was a justice of the peace, a well-known resident of that then small town, and had numerous sums in hand from farmers for investment. Our house was mortgaged and mother brought back the five hundred dollars which I handed over to Mr. Scott, who soon obtained for me the coveted ten shares in return. There was, unexpectedly, an additional hundred dollars to pay as a premium, but Mr. Scott kindly said I could pay that when convenient, and this of course was an easy matter to do.

This was my first investment. In those good old days monthly dividends were more plentiful than now and Adams Express paid a monthly dividend. One morning a white envelope was lying upon my desk, addressed in a big John Hancock hand, to "Andrew Carnegie, Esquire." "Esquire" tickled the boys and me inordinately. At one corner was seen the round stamp of Adams Express Company. I opened the envelope. All it contained was a check for ten dollars upon the Gold Exchange Bank of New York. I shall remember that check as long as I live, and that John Hancock signature of "J. C. Babcock, Cashier." It gave me the first penny of revenue from capital—something that I had not worked for with the sweat of my brow. "Eureka!" I cried. "Here's the goose that lays the golden eggs."

It was the custom of our party to spend Sunday afternoons in the woods. I kept the first check and showed it as we sat under the trees in a favorite grove we had found near Wood's Run. The effect produced

Pittsburgh before 1875.

Andrew Carnegie at twenty-four.

upon my companions was overwhelming. None of them had imagined such an investment possible. We resolved to save and to watch for the next opportunity for investment in which all of us should share, and for years afterward we divided our trifling investments and worked together almost as partners.

CHAPTER VII

A YOUNG SUPERINTENDENT

UP to this time my circle of acquaintances had not enlarged much. Mrs. Franciscus, wife of our freight agent, was very kind and on several occasions asked me to her house in Pittsburgh. She often spoke of the first time I rang the bell of the house in Third Street to deliver a message from Mr. Scott. She asked me to come in; I bashfully declined and it required coaxing upon her part to overcome my shyness. She was never able for years to induce me to partake of a meal in her house. I had great timidity about going into other people's houses, until late in life; but Mr. Scott would occasionally insist upon my going to his hotel and taking a meal with him, and these were great occasions for me. Mr. Franciscus's was the first considerable house, with the exception of Mr. Lombaert's at Altoona, I had ever entered, as far as I recollect. Every house was fashionable in my eyes that was upon any one of the principal streets, provided it had a hall entrance.

I had never spent a night in a strange house in my life until Mr. Stokes of Greensburg, chief counsel of the Pennsylvania Railroad, invited me to his beautiful home in the country to pass a Sunday. It was an odd thing for Mr. Stokes to do, for I could little interest a brilliant and educated man like him. The reason for my receiving such an honor was a communication I had written for the *Pittsburgh Journal*. Even in my teens I was a scribbler for the press. To be an editor was one of my ambitions. Horace Greeley and the

Tribune was my ideal of human triumph. Strange that there should have come a day when I could have bought the *Tribune*; but by that time the pearl had lost its luster. Our air castles are often within our grasp late in life, but then they charm not.

The subject of my article was upon the attitude of the city toward the Pennsylvania Railroad Company. It was signed anonymously and I was surprised to find it got a prominent place in the columns of the *Journal*, then owned and edited by Robert M. Riddle. I, as operator, received a telegram addressed to Mr. Scott and signed by Mr. Stokes, asking him to ascertain from Mr. Riddle who the author of that communication was. I knew that Mr. Riddle could not tell the author, because he did not know him; but at the same time I was afraid that if Mr. Scott called upon him he would hand him the manuscript, which Mr. Scott would certainly recognize at a glance. I therefore made a clean breast of it to Mr. Scott and told him I was the author. He seemed incredulous. He said he had read it that morning and wondered who had written it. His incredulous look did not pass me unnoticed. The pen was getting to be a weapon with me. Mr. Stokes's invitation to spend Sunday with him followed soon after, and the visit is one of the bright spots in my life. Henceforth we were great friends.

The grandeur of Mr. Stokes's home impressed me, but the one feature of it that eclipsed all else was a marble mantel in his library. In the center of the arch, carved in the marble, was an open book with this inscription:

> "He that cannot reason is a fool,
> He that will not, a bigot,
> He that dare not, a slave."

These noble words thrilled me. I said to myself, "Some day, some day, I'll have a library" (that was a look ahead) "and these words shall grace the mantel as here." And so they do in New York and Skibo to-day.

Mr. Scott was promoted to be the general superintendent of the Pennsylvania Railroad in 1856, taking Mr. Lombaert's place; and he took me, then in my twenty-third year, with him to Altoona. This breaking up of associations in Pittsburgh was a sore trial, but nothing could be allowed to interfere for a moment with my business career. My mother was satisfied upon this point, great as the strain was upon her. Besides, "follow my leader" was due to so true a friend as Mr. Scott had been.

The chief happening, judged by its consequences, of the two years I spent with Mr. Scott at Altoona, arose from my being the principal witness in a suit against the company, which was being tried at Greensburg by the brilliant Major Stokes, my first host. It was feared that I was about to be subpœnaed by the plaintiff, and the Major, wishing a postponement of the case, asked Mr. Scott to send me out of the State as rapidly as possible. This was a happy change for me, as I was enabled to visit my two bosom companions, Miller and Wilson, then in the railway service at Crestline, Ohio. On my way thither, while sitting on the end seat of the rear car watching the line, a farmer-looking man approached me. He carried a small green bag in his hand. He said the brakeman had informed him I was connected with the Pennsylvania Railroad. He wished to show me the model of a car which he had invented for night traveling. He took a small model out of the bag, which showed a section of a sleeping-car.

This was the celebrated T. T. Woodruff, the inventor of the sleeping-car. Its importance flashed upon me. I asked him if he would come to Altoona if I sent for him, and I promised to lay the matter before Mr. Scott at once upon my return. I could not get that sleeping-car idea out of my mind, and was most anxious to return to Altoona that I might press my views upon Mr. Scott. When I did so, he thought I was taking time by the forelock, but was quite receptive and said I might telegraph for the patentee. He came and contracted to place two of his cars upon the line as soon as they could be built. After this Mr. Woodruff, greatly to my surprise, asked me if I would not join him in the new enterprise and offered me an eighth interest in the venture.

I promptly accepted his offer, trusting to be able to make payments somehow or other. The two cars were to be paid for by monthly installments after delivery. When the time came for making the first payment, my portion was two hundred and seventeen and a half dollars. I boldly decided to apply to the local banker for a loan of that sum. I explained the matter to him, and I remember that he put his great arm (he was six feet three or four) around me, saying:

"Why, of course I will lend it. You are all right, Andy."

And here I made my first note, and actually got a banker to take it. A proud moment that in a young man's career! The sleeping-cars were a great success and their monthly receipts paid the monthly installments. The first considerable sum I made was from this source.

One important change in our life at Altoona, after my mother and brother arrived, was that, instead of continuing to live exclusively by ourselves, it was considered necessary that we should have a servant. It was with the greatest reluctance my mother could be brought to admit a stranger into the family circle. She had been everything and had done everything for her two boys. This was her life, and she resented the introduction of a stranger who was to be permitted to do anything whatever in the home. She had cooked and served her boys, washed their clothes and mended them, made their beds, cleaned their home. Who dare rob her of those motherly privileges! But nevertheless we could not escape the inevitable servant girl. One came, and others followed, and with these came also the destruction of much of that genuine family happiness which flows from exclusiveness. Being served by others is a poor substitute for a mother's labor of love. The ostentatious meal prepared by a strange cook whom one seldom sees, and served by hands paid for the task, lacks the sweetness of that which a mother's hands lay before you as the expression and proof of her devotion.

Among the manifold blessings I have to be thankful for is that neither nurse nor governess was my companion in infancy. No wonder the children of the poor are distinguished for the warmest affection and the closest adherence to family ties and are characterized by a filial regard far stronger than that of those who are mistakenly called more fortunate in life. They have passed the impressionable years of childhood and youth in constant loving contact with father and mother, to each they are all in all, no third person coming between. The child that has in his father a teacher, companion, and counselor, and whose mother is to him a nurse, seamstress, governess, teacher, companion, heroine, and saint all in one, has a heritage to which the child of wealth remains a stranger.

There comes a time, although the fond mother cannot see it, when a grown son has to put his arms around his saint and kissing her tenderly try to explain to her that it would be much better were she to let him help her in some ways; that, being out in the world among men and dealing with affairs, he sometimes sees changes which it would be desirable to make; that the mode of life delightful for young boys should be changed in some respects and the house made suitable for their friends to enter. Especially should the slaving mother live the life of ease hereafter, reading and visiting more and entertaining dear friends—in short, rising to her proper and deserved position as Her Ladyship.

Of course the change was very hard upon my mother, but she finally recognized the necessity for it, probably realized for the first time that her eldest son was getting on. "Dear Mother," I pleaded, my arms still around her, "you have done everything for and have been everything to Tom and me, and now do let me do something for you; let us be partners and let us always think what is best for each other. The time has come for you to play the lady and some of these days you are to ride in your carriage; meanwhile do get that girl in to help you. Tom and I would like this."

The victory was won, and my mother began to go out with us and visit her neighbors. She had not to learn self-possession nor good manners, these were innate; and as for education, knowledge, rare good sense, and kindliness, seldom was she to meet her equal. I wrote "never" instead of "seldom" and then struck it out. Nevertheless my private opinion is reserved.

Mr. Scott remained at Altoona for about three years when deserved promotion came to him. In 1859 he was made vice-president of the company, with his office in Philadelphia. What was to become of me was a serious question. Would he take me with him or must I remain at Altoona with the new official? The thought was to me unbearable. To part with Mr. Scott was hard enough; to serve a new official in his place I did not believe possible. The sun rose and set upon his head so far as I was concerned. The thought of my promotion, except through him, never entered my mind.

He returned from his interview with the president at Philadelphia and asked me to come into the private room in his house which communicated with the office. He told me it had been settled that he should remove to Philadelphia. Mr. Enoch Lewis, the division superintendent, was to be his successor. I listened with great interest as he approached the inevitable disclosure as to what he was going to do with me. He said finally:

"Now about yourself. Do you think you could manage the Pittsburgh Division?"

I was at an age when I thought I could manage anything. I knew nothing that I would not attempt, but it had never occurred to me that anybody else, much less Mr. Scott, would entertain the idea that I was as yet fit to do anything of the kind proposed. I was only twenty-four years old, but my model then was Lord John Russell, of whom it was said he would take the command of the Channel Fleet to-morrow. So would Wallace or Bruce. I told Mr. Scott I thought I could.

"Well," he said, "Mr. Potts" (who was then superintendent of the Pittsburgh Division) "is to be promoted to the transportation department in Philadelphia and I recommended you to the president as his successor. He agreed to give you a trial. What salary do you think you should have?"

"Salary," I said, quite offended; "what do I care for salary? I do not want the salary; I want the position. It is glory enough to go back to the Pittsburgh Division in your former place. You can make my salary just what you please and you need not give me any more than what I am getting now."

That was sixty-five dollars a month.

"You know," he said, "I received fifteen hundred dollars a year when I was there; and Mr. Potts is receiving eighteen hundred. I think it would be right to start you at fifteen hundred dollars, and after a while if you succeed you will get the eighteen hundred. Would that be satisfactory?"

"Oh, please," I said, "don't speak to me of money!"

It was not a case of mere hire and salary, and then and there my promotion was sealed. I was to have a department to myself, and instead of signing "T. A. S." orders between Pittsburgh and Altoona would now be signed "A. C." That was glory enough for me.

The order appointing me superintendent of the Pittsburgh Division was issued December 1, 1859. Preparations for removing the family were made at once. The change was hailed with joy, for although our residence in Altoona had many advantages, especially as we had a large house with some ground about it in a pleasant part of the suburbs and therefore many of the pleasures of country life, all these did not weigh as a feather in the scale as against the return to old friends and associations in dirty, smoky Pittsburgh. My brother Tom had learned telegraphy during his residence in Altoona and he returned with me and became my secretary.

The winter following my appointment was one of the most severe ever known. The line was poorly constructed, the equipment inefficient and totally inadequate for the business that was crowding upon it. The rails were laid upon huge blocks of stone, cast-iron chairs for holding the rails were used, and I have known as many as forty-seven of these to break in one night. No wonder the wrecks were frequent. The superintendent of a division in those days was expected to run trains by telegraph at night, to go out and remove all wrecks, and indeed to do everything. At one time for eight days I was constantly upon the line, day and night, at one wreck or obstruction after another. I was probably the most inconsiderate superintendent that ever was entrusted with the management of a great property, for, never knowing fatigue myself, being kept up by a sense of responsibility probably, I overworked the men and was not careful enough in considering the limits of human endurance. I have always been able to sleep at any time. Snatches of half an hour at intervals during the night in a dirty freight car were sufficient.

Upon our return to Pittsburgh in 1860 we rented a house in Hancock Street, now Eighth Street, and resided there for a year or more. Any accurate description of Pittsburgh at that time would be set down as a piece of the grossest exaggeration. The smoke permeated and penetrated everything. If you placed your hand on the balustrade of the stair it came away black; if you washed face and hands they were as dirty as ever in an hour. The soot gathered in the hair and irritated the skin, and for a time after our return from the mountain atmosphere of Altoona, life was more or less miserable. We soon began to consider how we could get to the country, and fortunately at that time Mr. D. A. Stewart, then freight agent for the company, directed our attention to a house adjoining his residence at

Homewood. We moved there at once and the telegraph was brought in, which enabled me to operate the division from the house when necessary.

Here a new life was opened to us. There were country lanes and gardens in abundance. Residences had from five to twenty acres of land about them. The Homewood Estate was made up of many hundreds of acres, with beautiful woods and glens and a running brook. We, too, had a garden and a considerable extent of ground around our house. The happiest years of my mother's life were spent here among her flowers and chickens and the surroundings of country life. Her love of flowers was a passion. She was scarcely ever able to gather a flower. Indeed I remember she once reproached me for pulling up a weed, saying "it was something green." I have inherited this peculiarity and have often walked from the house to the gate intending to pull a flower for my button-hole and then left for town unable to find one I could destroy.

With this change to the country came a whole host of new acquaintances. Many of the wealthy families of the district had their residences in this delightful suburb. It was, so to speak, the aristocratic quarter. To the entertainments at these great houses the young superintendent was invited. The young people were musical and we had musical evenings a plenty. I heard subjects discussed which I had never known before, and I made it a rule when I heard these to learn something about them at once. I was pleased every day to feel that I was learning something new.

I began to pay strict attention to my language, and to the English classics, which I now read with great avidity. I began also to notice how much better it was to be gentle in tone and manner, polite and courteous to all—in short, better behaved. Up to this time I had been, perhaps, careless in dress and rather affected it. Great heavy boots, loose collar, and general roughness of attire were then peculiar to the West and in our circle considered manly. Anything that could be labeled foppish was looked upon with contempt. I remember the first gentleman I ever saw in the service of the railway company who wore kid gloves. He was the object of derision among us who aspired to be manly men. I was a great deal the better in all these respects after we moved to Homewood.

CHAPTER VIII

AT THE OLD HOME

IN 1861 the Civil War broke out and I was at once summoned to Washington by Mr. Scott, who had been appointed Assistant Secretary of War in charge of the Transportation Department. I was to act as his assistant in charge of the military railroads and telegraphs of the Government and to organize a force of railway men. It was one of the most important departments of all at the beginning of the war.

The first regiments of Union troops passing through Baltimore had been attacked, and the railway line cut between Baltimore and Annapolis Junction, destroying communication with Washington. It was therefore necessary for me, with my corps of assistants, to take train at Philadelphia for Annapolis, a point from which a branch line extended to the Junction, joining the main line to Washington. Our first duty was to repair this branch and make it passable for heavy trains, a work of some days. General Butler and several regiments of troops arrived a few days after us, and we were able to transport his whole brigade to Washington.

I took my place upon the first engine which started for the Capital, and proceeded very cautiously. Some distance from Washington I noticed that the telegraph wires had been pinned to the ground by wooden stakes. I stopped the engine and ran forward to release them, but I did not notice that the wires had been pulled to one side before staking. When released, in their spring upwards, they struck me in the face, knocked me over, and cut a gash in my cheek which bled profusely. In this condition I entered the city of Washington with the first troops, so that with the exception of one or two soldiers, wounded a few days previously in passing through the streets of Baltimore, I can justly claim that I "shed my blood for my country" among the first of its defenders. I gloried in being useful to the land that had done so much for me, and worked, I can truly say, night and day, to open communication to the South.

Soon after this I returned to Washington and made my headquarters in the War Building with Colonel Scott. As I had charge of the telegraph department, as well as the railways, this gave me an opportunity of seeing President Lincoln, Mr. Seward, Secretary Cameron, and others; and I was occasionally brought in personal contact with these men, which was to me a source of great interest. Mr. Lincoln would occasionally come to the office and sit at the desk awaiting replies to telegrams, or perhaps merely anxious for information.

All the pictures of this extraordinary man are like him. He was so marked of feature that it was impossible for any one to paint him and not produce a likeness. He was certainly one of the most homely men I ever saw when his features were in repose; but when excited or telling a story, intellect shone through his eyes and illuminated his face to a degree which I have seldom or never seen in any other. His manners were perfect because natural; and he had a kind word for everybody, even the youngest boy in the office. His attentions were not graduated. They were the same to all, as deferential in talking to the messenger boy as to Secretary Seward. His charm lay in the total absence of manner. It was not so much, perhaps, what he said as the way in which he said it that never failed to win one. I have often regretted that I did not note down carefully at the time some of his curious sayings, for he said even common things in an original way. I never met a great man who so thoroughly made himself one with all men as Mr. Lincoln.

When I was called to Washington in 1861, it was supposed that the war would soon be over; but it was seen shortly afterwards that it was to be a question of years. Permanent officials in charge would be required. The Pennsylvania Railroad Company was unable to spare Mr. Scott, and Mr. Scott, in turn, decided that I must return to Pittsburgh, where my services were urgently needed, owing to the demands made upon the Pennsylvania by the Government. We therefore placed the department at Washington in the hands of others and returned to our respective positions.

After my return from Washington reaction followed and I was taken with my first serious illness. I was completely broken down, and after a struggle to perform my duties was compelled to seek rest. One afternoon, when on the railway line in Virginia, I had experienced something like a sunstroke, which gave me considerable trouble. It passed off, however, but after that I found I could not stand heat and had to be careful to keep out of the sun—a hot day wilting me completely.

Leave of absence was granted me by the Pennsylvania Railroad Company, and the long-sought opportunity to visit Scotland came. My mother, my bosom friend Tom Miller, and myself, sailed in the steamship Etna,

June 28, 1862, I in my twenty-seventh year; and on landing in Liverpool we proceeded at once to Dunfermline. No change ever affected me so much as this return to my native land. I seemed to be in a dream. Every mile that brought us nearer to Scotland increased the intensity of my feelings. My mother was equally moved, and I remember, when her eyes first caught sight of the familiar yellow bush, she exclaimed:

"Oh! there's the broom, the broom!"

Her heart was so full she could not restrain her tears, and the more I tried to make light of it or to soothe her, the more she was overcome. For myself, I felt as if I could throw myself upon the sacred soil and kiss it.

In this mood we reached Dunfermline. Every object we passed was recognized at once, but everything seemed so small, compared with what I had imagined it, that I was completely puzzled. Finally, reaching Uncle Lauder's and getting into the old room where he had taught Dod and myself so many things, I exclaimed:

"You are all here; everything is just as I left it, but you are now all playing with toys."

The High Street, which I had considered not a bad Broadway, uncle's shop, which I had compared with some New York establishments, the little mounds about the town, to which we had run on Sundays to play, the distances, the height of the houses, all had shrunk. Here was a city of the Lilliputians. I could almost touch the eaves of the house in which I was born, and the sea—to walk to which on a Saturday had been considered quite a feat—was only three miles distant. The rocks at the seashore, among which I had gathered wilks (whelks) seemed to have vanished, and a tame flat shoal remained. The schoolhouse, around which

'The Carnegie Demonstration of 1881' painting by Blair & Geddes — when his mother laid the foundation stone of the Dunfermline Library.

The Edgar Thomson Steel Works at Braddock, Pennsylvania (see p. 79).

The Lucy Furnace (see p. 98).

had centered many of my schoolboy recollections—my only Alma Mater—and the playground, upon which mimic battles had been fought and races run, had shrunk into ridiculously small dimensions. The fine residences, and especially the conservatories at Donibristle, fell one after the other into the petty and insignificant. What I felt on a later occasion on a visit to Japan, with its small toy houses, was something like a repetition of the impression my old home made upon me.

Everything was there in miniature. Even the old well at the head of Moodie Street, where I began my early struggles, was changed from what I had pictured it. But one object remained all that I had dreamed of it. There was no disappointment in the glorious old Abbey and its Glen. It was big enough and grand enough, and the memorable carved letters on the top of the tower—"King Robert The Bruce"—filled my eye and my heart as fully as of old. Nor was the Abbey bell disappointing, when I heard it for the first time after my return. For this I was grateful. It gave me a rallying point, and around the old Abbey, with its Palace ruins and the Glen, other objects adjusted themselves in their true proportions after a time.

My relatives were exceedingly kind, and the oldest of all, my dear old Auntie Charlotte, in a moment of exultation exclaimed:

"Oh, you will just be coming back here some day and *keep a shop in the High Street*."

To keep a shop in the High Street was her idea of triumph. Her son-in-law and daughter, both my full cousins, though unrelated to each other, had risen to this sublime height, and nothing was too great to predict for her promising nephew. There is an aristocracy even in shopkeeping, and the family of the green-grocer of the High Street mingles not upon equal terms with him of Moodie Street.

Auntie, who had often played my nurse, liked to dwell upon the fact that I was a screaming infant that had to be fed with two spoons, as I yelled whenever one left my mouth. Captain Jones, our superintendent of the steel works at a later day, described me as having been born "with two rows of teeth and holes punched for more," so insatiable was my appetite for new works and increased production. As I was the first child in our immediate family circle, there were plenty of now venerable relatives begging to be allowed to play nurse, my aunties among them. Many of my childhood pranks and words they told me in their old age. One of them that the aunties remembered struck me as rather precocious.

I had been brought up upon wise saws and one that my father had taught me was soon given direct application. As a boy, returning from the seashore three miles distant, he had to carry me part of the way upon his back. Going up a steep hill in the gloaming he remarked upon the heavy load, hoping probably I would propose to walk a bit. The response, however, which he received was:

"Ah, faither, never mind, patience and perseverance make the man, ye ken."

He toiled on with his burden, but shaking with laughter. He was hoist with his own petard, but his burden grew lighter all the same. I am sure of this.

My home, of course, was with my instructor, guide, and inspirer, Uncle Lauder—he who had done so much to make me romantic, patriotic, and poetical at eight. Now I was twenty-seven, but Uncle Lauder still remained Uncle Lauder. He had not shrunk, no one could fill his place. We had our walks and talks constantly and I was "Naig" again to him. He had never had any name for me but that and never did have. My dear, dear uncle, and more, much more than uncle to me.

I was still dreaming and so excited that I could not sleep and had caught cold in the bargain. The natural result of this was a fever. I lay in uncle's house for six weeks, a part of that time in a critical condition. Scottish medicine was stern, and I was bled. My thin American blood was so depleted that when I was pronounced convalescent it was long before I could stand upon my feet. This illness put an end to my visit, but by the time I had reached America again, the ocean voyage had done me so much good I was able to resume work.

I remember being deeply affected by the reception I met with when I returned to my division. The men of the eastern end gathered together with a cannon and while the train passed I was greeted with a salvo. This was perhaps the first occasion upon which my subordinates had an opportunity of making me the subject of any demonstration, and their reception made a lasting impression. I knew how much I cared for them and it was pleasing to know that they reciprocated my feelings. Working-men always do reciprocate kindly feeling. If we truly care for others we need not be anxious about their feelings for us. Like draws to like.

CHAPTER IX

BRIDGE-BUILDING

DURING the Civil War the price of iron went up to something like $130 per ton. Even at that figure it was not so much a question of money as of delivery. The railway lines of America were fast becoming dangerous for want of new rails, and this state of affairs led me to organize in 1864 a rail-making concern at Pittsburgh. There was no difficulty in obtaining partners and capital, and the Superior Rail Mill and Blast Furnaces were built.

In like manner the demand for locomotives was very great, and with Mr. Thomas N. Miller I organized in 1866 the Pittsburgh Locomotive Works, which has been a prosperous and creditable concern—locomotives made there having obtained an enviable reputation throughout the United States. It sounds like a fairy tale to-day to record that in 1906 the one-hundred-dollar shares of this company sold for three thousand dollars—that is, thirty dollars for one. Large annual dividends had been paid regularly and the company had been very successful—sufficient proof of the policy: "Make nothing but the very best." We never did.

When at Altoona I had seen in the Pennsylvania Railroad Company's works the first small bridge built of iron. It proved a success. I saw that it would never do to depend further upon wooden bridges for permanent railway structures. An important bridge on the Pennsylvania Railroad had recently burned and the traffic had been obstructed for eight days. Iron was the thing. I proposed to H. J. Linville, who had designed the iron bridge, and to John L. Piper and his partner, Mr. Schiffler, who had charge of bridges on the Pennsylvania line, that they should come to Pittsburgh and I would organize a company to build iron bridges. It was the first company of its kind. I asked my friend, Mr. Scott, of the Pennsylvania Railroad, to go with us in the venture, which he did. Each of us paid for a one fifth interest, or $1250. My share I borrowed from the bank. Looking back at it now the sum seemed very small, but "tall oaks from little acorns grow."

In this way was organized in 1862 the firm of Piper and Schiffler which was merged into the Keystone Bridge Company in 1863—a name which I remember I was proud of having thought of as being most appropriate for a bridge-building concern in the State of Pennsylvania, the Keystone State. From this beginning iron bridges came generally into use in America, indeed, in the world at large so far as I know. My letters to iron manufacturers in Pittsburgh were sufficient to insure the new company credit. Small wooden shops were erected and several bridge structures were undertaken. Cast-iron was the principal material used, but so well were the bridges built that some made at that day and since strengthened for heavier traffic, still remain in use upon various lines.

The Keystone Bridge Works have always been a source of satisfaction to me. Almost every concern that had undertaken to erect iron bridges in America had failed. Many of the structures themselves had fallen and some of the worst railway disasters in America had been caused in that way. Some of the bridges had given way under wind pressure but nothing has ever happened to a Keystone bridge, and some of them have stood where the wind was not tempered. There has been no luck about it. We used only the best material and enough of it, making our own iron and later our own steel. We were our own severest inspectors, and would build a safe structure or none at all. When asked to build a bridge which we knew to be of insufficient strength or of unscientific design, we resolutely declined. Any piece of work bearing the stamp of the Keystone Bridge Works (and there are few States in the Union where such are not to be found) we were prepared to underwrite. We were as proud of our bridges as Carlyle was of the bridge his father built across the Annan. "An honest brig," as the great son rightly said.

This policy is the true secret of success. Uphill work it will be for a few years until your work is proven, but after that it is smooth sailing. Instead of objecting to inspectors they should be welcomed by all manufacturing establishments. A high standard of excellence is easily maintained, and men are educated in the effort to reach excellence. I have never known a concern to make a decided success that did not do good, honest work, and even in these days of the fiercest competition, when everything would seem to be matter of price, there lies still at the root of great business success the very much more important factor of quality. The effect of attention to quality, upon every man in the service, from the president of the concern down to the humblest laborer, cannot be overestimated. The surest foundation of a manufacturing concern is quality. After that, and a long way after, comes cost. And bearing on the same question, clean, fine workshops and tools, well-kept yards and surroundings are of much greater importance than is usually supposed.

I was very much pleased to hear a remark, made by one of the prominent bankers who visited the Edgar Thomson Works during a Bankers' Convention held at Pittsburgh. He was one of a party of some hundreds of delegates, and after they had passed through the works he said to our manager:

"Somebody appears to belong to these works."

He put his finger there upon one of the secrets of success. They did belong to somebody. The president of an important manufacturing work once boasted to me that their men had chased away the first inspector who had ventured to appear among them, and that they had never been troubled with another since. This was said as a matter of sincere congratulation, but I thought to myself: "This concern will never stand the strain of competition; it is bound to fail when hard times come." The result proved the correctness of my belief.

I gave a great deal of personal attention for some years to the affairs of the Keystone Bridge Works, and when important contracts were involved often went myself to meet the parties. On one such occasion in 1868, I visited Dubuque, Iowa, with our engineer. We were competing for the building of the most important railway bridge that had been built up to that time, a bridge across the wide Mississippi at Dubuque, to span which was considered a great undertaking. We found the river frozen and crossed it upon a sleigh drawn by four horses.

That visit proved how much success turns upon trifles. We found we were not the lowest bidder. Our chief rival was a bridge-building concern in Chicago to which the board had decided to award the contract.

I lingered and talked with some of the directors. They were delightfully ignorant of the merits of cast- and wrought-iron. We had always made the upper cord of the bridge of the latter, while our rivals' was made of cast-iron. This furnished my text. I pictured the result of a steamer striking against the one and against the other. In the case of the wrought-iron cord it would probably only bend; in the case of the cast-iron it would certainly break and down would come the bridge. One of the directors was fortunately able to enforce my argument, by stating to the board that what I said was undoubtedly the case about cast-iron. The other night he had run his buggy in the dark against a lamp-post which was of cast-iron and the lamp-post had broken to pieces.

"Ah, gentlemen," I said, "there is the point. A little more money and you could have had the indestructible wrought-iron and your bridge would stand against any steamboat. We never have built and we never will build a cheap bridge. Ours don't fall."

There was a pause; then the president of the bridge company asked if I would excuse them for a few moments. I retired. Soon they recalled me and offered the contract, provided we took the lower price, which was only a few thousand dollars less. I agreed to the concession. That cast-iron lamp-post so opportunely smashed gave us one of our most profitable contracts and, what is more, obtained for us the reputation of having taken the Dubuque bridge against all competitors.

The moral of that story lies on the surface. If you want a contract, be on the spot when it is let. A smashed lamp-post or something equally unthought of may secure the prize if the bidder be on hand. And if possible stay on hand until you can take the written contract home in your pocket. This we did at Dubuque, although it was suggested we could leave and it would be sent after us to execute. We preferred to remain, being anxious to see more of the charms of Dubuque.

After building the Steubenville Bridge, it became a necessity for the Baltimore and Ohio Railroad Company to build bridges across the Ohio River at Parkersburg and Wheeling, to prevent their great rival, the Pennsylvania Railroad Company, from possessing a decided advantage. The days of ferry-boats were then fast passing away. It was in connection with the contracts for these bridges that I had the pleasure of making the acquaintance of a man, then of great position, Mr. Garrett, president of the Baltimore and Ohio.

We were most anxious to secure both bridges and all the approaches to them, but I found Mr. Garrett decidedly of the opinion that we were quite unable to do so much work in the time specified. He wished to build the approaches and the short spans in his own shops, and asked me if we would permit him to use our patents. I replied that we would feel highly honored by the Baltimore and Ohio doing so. The stamp of approval of the Baltimore and Ohio Railroad would be worth ten times the patent fees. He could use all, and everything, we had.

There was no doubt as to the favorable impression that made upon the great railway magnate. He was much pleased and, to my utter surprise, took me into his private room and opened up a frank conversation upon matters in general. He touched especially upon his quarrels with the Pennsylvania Railroad people, with Mr. Thomson and Mr. Scott, the president and vice-president, whom he knew to be my special friends.

This led me to say that I had passed through Philadelphia on my way to see him and had been asked by Mr. Scott where I was going.

"I told him that I was going to visit you to obtain the contracts for your great bridges over the Ohio River. Mr. Scott said it was not often that I went on a fool's errand, but that I was certainly on one now; that Mr. Garrett would never think for a moment of giving me his contracts, for every one knew that I was, as a former employee, always friendly to the Pennsylvania Railroad. Well, I said, we shall build Mr. Garrett's bridges."

Mr. Garrett promptly replied that when the interests of his company were at stake it was the best always that won. His engineers had reported that our plans were the best and that Scott and Thomson would see that he had only one rule—the interests of his company. Although he very well knew that I was a Pennsylvania Railroad man, yet he felt it his duty to award us the work.

The negotiation was still unsatisfactory to me, because we were to get all the difficult part of the work —the great spans of which the risk was then considerable —while Mr. Garrett was to build all the small and profitable spans at his own shops upon our plans and patents. I ventured to ask whether he was dividing the work because he honestly believed we could not open his bridges for traffic as soon as his masonry would permit. He admitted he was. I told him that he need not have any fear upon that point.

"Mr. Garrett," I said, "would you consider my personal bond a good security?"

"Certainly," he said.

"Well, now," I replied, "bind me! I know what I

am doing. I will take the risk. How much of a bond do you want me to give you that your bridges will be opened for traffic at the specified time if you give us the entire contract, provided you get your masonry ready?"

"Well, I would want a hundred thousand dollars from you, young man."

"All right," I said, "prepare your bond. Give us the work. Our firm is not going to let me lose a hundred thousand dollars. You know that."

"Yes," he said, "I believe if you are bound for a hundred thousand dollars your company will work day and night and I will get my bridges."

This was the arrangement which gave us what were then the gigantic contracts of the Baltimore and Ohio Railroad. It is needless to say that I never had to pay that bond. My partners knew much better than Mr. Garrett the conditions of his work. The Ohio River was not to be trifled with, and long before his masonry was ready we had relieved ourselves from all responsibility upon the bond by placing the superstructure on the banks awaiting the completion of the substructure which he was still building.

CHAPTER X

THE IRON WORKS

THE Keystone Works have always been my pet as being the parent of all the other works. But they had not been long in existence before the advantage of wrought- over cast-iron became manifest. Accordingly, to insure uniform quality, and also to make certain shapes which were not then to be obtained, we determined to embark in the manufacture of iron. My brother and I became interested with Thomas N. Miller, Henry Phipps, and Andrew Kloman in a small iron mill.

Andrew Kloman had a small steel-hammer in Allegheny City. As a superintendent of the Pennsylvania Railroad I had found that he made the best axles. He was a great mechanic—one who had discovered, what was then unknown in Pittsburgh, that whatever was worth doing with machinery was worth doing well. His German mind made him thorough. What he constructed cost enormously, but when once started it did the work it was intended to do from year's end to year's end. In those early days it was a question with axles generally whether they would run any specified time or break. There was no analysis of material, no scientific treatment of it.

How much this German created! He was the first man to introduce the cold saw that cut cold iron the exact length. He invented upsetting machines to make bridge links, and also built the first "universal" mill in America. All these were erected at our works. When Captain Eads could not obtain the couplings for the St. Louis Bridge arches (the contractors failing to make them) and matters were at a standstill, Kloman told us that he could make them and why the others had failed. He succeeded in making them. Up to that date they were the largest semicircles that had ever been rolled. Our confidence in Mr. Kloman may be judged from the fact that when he said he could make them we unhesitatingly contracted to furnish them.

Unfortunately Kloman and Phipps soon differed with Miller about the business and forced him out. Being convinced that Miller was unfairly treated, I united with him in building new works. These were the Cyclops Mills of 1864. After they were set running it became possible, and therefore advisable, to unite the old and the new works, and the Union Iron Mills were formed by their consolidation in 1867.

We began at the new mill by making all shapes which were required, and especially such as no other concern would undertake, depending upon an increasing demand in our growing country for things that were only rarely needed at first. What others could not or would not do we would attempt, and this was a rule of our business which was strictly adhered to. Also we would make nothing except of excellent quality. We always accommodated our customers, even although at some expense to ourselves, and in cases of dispute we gave the other party the benefit of the doubt and settled. These were our rules. We had no lawsuits.

As I became acquainted with the manufacture of iron I was greatly surprised to find that the cost of each of the various processes was unknown. Inquiries made of the leading manufacturers of Pittsburgh proved this.

It was a lump business, and until stock was taken and the books balanced at the end of the year, the manufacturers were in total ignorance of results. I heard of men who thought their business at the end of the year would show a loss and had found a profit, and *vice-versa*. I felt as if we were moles burrowing in the dark, and this to me was intolerable. I insisted upon such a system of weighing and accounting being introduced throughout our works as would enable us to know what our cost was for each process and especially what each man was doing, who saved material, who wasted it, and who produced the best results.

To arrive at this was a much more difficult task than one would imagine. Every manager in the mills was naturally against the new system. Years were required before an accurate system was obtained, but eventually, by the aid of many clerks and the introduction of weighing scales at various points in the mill, we began to know not only what every department was doing, but what each one of the many men working at the furnaces was doing, and thus to compare one with another. One of the chief sources of success in manufacturing is the introduction and strict maintenance of a perfect system of accounting so that responsibility for money or materials can be brought home to every man. Owners who, in the office, would not trust a clerk with five dollars without having a check upon him, were supplying tons of material daily to men in the mills without exacting an account of their stewardship by weighing what each returned in the finished form.

My investments now began to require so much of my personal attention that I resolved to leave the service of the railway company and devote myself exclusively to my own affairs. I had been honored a short time before this decision by being called by President Thomson to Philadelphia. He desired to promote me to the office of assistant general superintendent with headquarters at Altoona under Mr. Lewis. I declined, telling him that I had decided to give up the railroad service altogether, that I was determined to make a fortune and I saw no means of doing this honestly at any salary the railroad company could afford to give, and I would not do it by indirection. When I lay down at night I was going to get a verdict of approval from the highest of all tribunals, the judge within.

I repeated this in my parting letter to President Thomson, who warmly congratulated me upon it in his letter of reply. I resigned my position March 28, 1865, and received from the men on the railway a gold watch. This and Mr. Thomson's letter I treasure among my most precious mementos.

The following letter was written to the men on the Division:

PENNSYLVANIA RAILROAD COMPANY
SUPERINTENDENT'S OFFICE, PITTSBURGH DIVISION
PITTSBURGH, *March* 28, 1865

To the Officers and Employees of the Pittsburgh Division.

GENTLEMEN:

I cannot allow my connection with you to cease without some expression of the deep regret felt at parting.

Twelve years of pleasant intercourse have served to inspire feelings of personal regard for those who have so faithfully labored with me in the service of the Company. The coming change is painful only as I reflect that in consequence thereof I am not to be in the future, as in the past, intimately associated with you and with many others in the various departments, who have through business intercourse, become my personal friends. I assure you although the official relations hitherto existing between us must soon close, I can never fail to feel and evince the liveliest interest in the welfare of such as have been identified with the Pittsburgh Division in times past, and who are, I trust, for many years to come to contribute to the success of the Pennsylvania Railroad Company, and share in its justly deserved prosperity.

Thanking you most sincerely for the uniform kindness shown toward me, for your zealous efforts made at all times to meet my wishes, and asking for my successor similar support at your hands, I bid you all farewell.

Very respectfully

(Signed) ANDREW CARNEGIE

In the year 1867, Mr. Phipps, Mr. J. W. Vandevort, and myself revisited Europe, traveling extensively through England and Scotland, and made the tour of the Continent. We visited most of the capitals of Europe, and in all the enthusiasm of youth climbed every spire, slept on mountain-tops, and carried our luggage in knapsacks upon our backs. We ended our journey upon Vesuvius, where we resolved some day to go around the world.

This visit to Europe proved most instructive. Up to this time I had known nothing of painting or sculpture, but it was not long before I could classify the works of the great painters. One may not at the time justly appreciate the advantage he is receiving from examining

Pittencrieff Park, Dunfermline.

Dec 68
St Nicholas
Hotel report

Thirty three and an income of 50,000$
per annum,
By this time two years I can so arrange all
my business as to secure at least 50,000 per
annum — Beyond this never earn — make no
effort to increase fortune, but spend the
surplus each year for benevolent purposes,
Cast aside business forever except for
others, —
Settle in Oxford & get a thorough education
making the acquaintance of literary men
this will take three years active work —
pay especial attention to speaking in public,
Settle then in London & purchase a
controlling interest in some Newspaper or
live review & give the general management
of it attention, taking a part in public
matters especially those connected with
education & improvement of the poorer
classes —
Man must have an idol — The amassing
of wealth is one of the worst species of
idolatry — No idol more debasing than the
worship of money — Whatever I engage in I must
push inordinately therefor should I be careful
to choose that life which will be the most elevating
in its character — To continue much longer
overwhelmed by business cares and with most
of my thoughts wholly upon the way to make
more money in the shortest time, must degrade
me beyond hope of permanent recovery,
I will resign business at Thirty five, but during
the ensuing two years I wish to spend the afternoons
in receiving instruction, and in reading systematically

St. Nicholas Hotel Memorandum, 1868 (see p. 92).

the great masterpieces, but upon his return to America he will find himself unconsciously rejecting what before seemed truly beautiful, and judging productions which come before him by a new standard. That which is truly great has so impressed itself upon him that what is false or pretentious proves no longer attractive.

My visit to Europe also gave me my first great treat in music. The Handel Anniversary was then being celebrated at the Crystal Palace in London, and I had never up to that time, nor have I often since, felt the power and majesty of music in such high degree. What I heard at the Crystal Palace and what I subsequently heard on the Continent in the cathedrals, and at the opera, certainly enlarged my appreciation of music. At Rome the Pope's choir and the celebrations in the churches at Christmas and Easter furnished, as it were, a grand climax to the whole.

These visits to Europe were also of great service in a commercial sense. One has to get out of the swirl of the great Republic to form a just estimate of the velocity with which it spins. I felt that a manufacturing concern like ours could scarcely develop fast enough for the wants of the American people, but abroad nothing seemed to be going forward.

It was Cousin "Dod" (Mr. George Lauder) to whom we were indebted for a new development in our mill operations—the first of its kind in America. He it was who took our Mr. Coleman to Wigan in England and explained the process of washing and coking the dross from coal mines. Mr. Coleman had constantly been telling us how grand it would be to utilize what was then being thrown away at our mines, and was indeed an expense to dispose of. Our Cousin "Dod" was a mechanical engineer, educated under Lord Kelvin at

Glasgow University, and as he corroborated all that Mr. Coleman stated, in December, 1871, I undertook to advance the capital to build works along the line of the Pennsylvania Railroad. Contracts for ten years were made with the leading coal companies for their dross and with the railway companies for transportation, and Mr. Lauder, who came to Pittsburgh and superintended the whole operation for years, began the construction of the first coal-washing machinery in America. He made a success of it—he never failed to do that in any mining or mechanical operation he undertook—and he soon cleared the cost of the works. "Dod" had won his spurs.

The ovens were extended from time to time until we had five hundred of them, washing nearly fifteen hundred tons of coal daily. I confess I never pass these coal ovens at Larimer's Station without feeling that if he who makes two blades of grass grow where one grew before is a public benefactor and lays the race under obligation, those who produce superior coke from material that has been for all previous years thrown over the bank as worthless, have great cause for self-congratulation. It is fine to make something out of nothing; it is also something to be the first firm to do this upon our continent.

We had another valuable partner in a second cousin of mine, a son of Cousin Morrison of Dunfermline. Walking through the shops one day, the superintendent asked me if I knew I had a relative there who was proving an exceptional mechanic. I replied in the negative and asked that I might speak with him on our way around. We met. I asked his name.

"Morrison," was the reply, "son of Robert"—my cousin Bob.

"Well, how did you come here?"

"I thought we could better ourselves," he said.

"Who have you with you?"

"My wife," was the reply.

"Why didn't you come first to see your relative who might have been able to introduce you here?"

"Well, I didn't feel I needed help if I only got a chance."

There spoke the true Morrison, taught to depend on himself, and independent as Lucifer. Not long afterwards I heard of his promotion to the superintendency of our newly acquired works at Duquesne, and from that position he steadily marched upward. He is to-day a blooming, but still sensible, millionaire. We are all proud of Tom Morrison.

Our business continued to expand and required frequent visits on my part to the East, especially to New York, which is as London to Britain—the headquarters of all really important enterprises in America. No large concern could very well get on without being represented there. My brother and Mr. Phipps had full grasp of the business at Pittsburgh. My field appeared to be to direct the general policy of the companies and negotiate the important contracts.

I was once more compelled to break old association and leave Pittsburgh in 1867 to take up my residence in New York. The change was hard enough for me, but much harder for my mother; but she was still in the prime of life and we could be happy anywhere so long as we were together. Still she did feel the leaving of our home very much. We were perfect strangers in New York, and at first took up our quarters in the St. Nicholas Hotel, then in its glory. I opened an office in Broad Street.

The ambitions of Mr. Carnegie at this time (1868) are set forth in the following memorandum made by him. It has only recently come to light:

St. Nicholas Hotel, New York
December, 1868

Thirty-three and an income of $50,000 per annum! By this time two years I can so arrange all my business as to secure at least $50,000 per annum. Beyond this never earn—make no effort to increase fortune, but spend the surplus each year for benevolent purposes. Cast aside business forever, except for others.

Settle in Oxford and get a thorough education, making the acquaintance of literary men—this will take three years' active work—pay especial attention to speaking in public. Settle then in London and purchase a controlling interest in some newspaper or live review and give the general management of it attention, taking a part in public matters, especially those connected with education and improvement of the poorer classes.

Man must have an idol—the amassing of wealth is one of the worst species of idolatry—no idol more debasing than the worship of money. Whatever I engage in I must push inordinately; therefore should I be careful to choose that life which will be the most elevating in its character. To continue much longer overwhelmed by business cares and with most of my thoughts wholly upon the way to make more money in the shortest time, must degrade me beyond hope of permanent recovery. I will resign business at thirty-five, but during the ensuing two years I wish to spend the afternoons in receiving instruction and in reading systematically.

CHAPTER XI

HOW CARNEGIE DID BUSINESS

As an incident of my financial operations I remember saying to Mr. Junius S. Morgan one day:

"Mr. Morgan, I will give you an idea and help you to carry it forward if you will give me one quarter of all the money you make by acting upon it."

He laughingly said: "That seems fair, and as I have the option to act upon it, or not, certainly we ought to be willing to pay you a quarter of the profit."

I called attention to the fact that the Allegheny Valley Railway bonds which I had exchanged for the Philadelphia and Erie bonds bore the guarantee of the Pennsylvania Railroad Company, and that that great company was always in need of money for essential extensions. A price might be offered for these bonds which might tempt the company to sell them, and that at the moment there appeared to be such a demand for American securities that no doubt they could be floated. I would write a prospectus which I thought would float the bonds. After examining the matter with his usual care he decided that he would act upon my suggestion.

Mr. Thomson was then in Paris and I ran over there to see him. Knowing that the Pennsylvania Railroad had need for money I told him that I had recommended these securities to Mr. Morgan and if he would give me a price for them I would see if I could not sell them. He named a price which was then very high, but less than the price which these bonds have since reached.

Mr. Morgan purchased part of them with the right to buy others, and in this way the whole nine or ten millions of Allegheny bonds were marketed and the Pennsylvania Railroad Company placed in funds.

The sale of the bonds had not gone very far when the panic of 1873 was upon us. One of the sources of revenue which I then had was Mr. Pierpont Morgan. He said to me one day:

"My father has cabled to ask whether you wish to sell out your interest in that idea you gave him."

I said: "Yes, I do. In these days I will sell anything for money."

"Well," he said, "what would you take?"

I said I believed that a statement recently rendered to me showed that there were already fifty thousand dollars to my credit, and I would take sixty thousand. Next morning when I called Mr. Morgan handed me checks for seventy thousand dollars.

"Mr. Carnegie," he said, "you were mistaken. You sold out for ten thousand dollars less than the statement showed to your credit. It now shows not fifty but sixty thousand to your credit, and the additional ten makes seventy."

The payments were in two checks, one for sixty thousand dollars and the other for the additional ten thousand. I handed him back the ten-thousand-dollar check, saying:

"Well, that is something worthy of you. Will you please accept these ten thousand with my best wishes?"

"No, thank you," he said, "I cannot do that."

Such acts, showing a nice sense of honorable understanding as against mere legal rights, are not so uncommon in business as the uninitiated might believe. And, after that, it is not to be wondered at if I determined that so far as lay in my power neither Morgan, father or son, nor their house, should suffer through me. They had in me henceforth a firm friend.

A great business is seldom if ever built up, except on lines of the strictest integrity. A reputation for "cuteness" and sharp dealing is fatal in great affairs. Not the letter of the law, but the spirit, must be the rule. The standard of commercial morality is now very high. A mistake made by any one in favor of the firm is corrected as promptly as if the error were in favor of the other party. It is essential to permanent success that a house should obtain a reputation for being governed by what is fair rather than what is merely legal. A rule which we adopted and adhered to has given greater returns than one would believe possible, namely: always give the other party the benefit of the doubt.

I made repeated journeys to Europe to negotiate various securities, and in all I sold some thirty millions of dollars' worth. This was at a time when the Atlantic cable had not yet made New York a part of London financially considered, and when London bankers would lend their balances to Paris, Vienna, or Berlin for a shadow of difference in the rate of interest rather than to the United States at a higher rate. The Republic was considered less safe than the Continent by these good people. My brother and Mr. Phipps conducted the iron business so successfully that I could leave for weeks at a time without anxiety. There was danger lest I should drift away from the manufacturing to the financial and banking business. My successes abroad brought me tempting opportunities, but my preference was always for manufacturing. I wished to make something tangible and sell it and I continued to invest my profits in extending the works at Pittsburgh.

The small shops put up originally for the Keystone Bridge Company had been leased for other purposes and ten acres of ground had been secured in Lawrenceville on which new and extensive shops were erected. Repeated additions to the Union Iron Mills had made them the leading mills in the United States for all sorts of structural shapes. Business was promising and all the surplus earnings I was making in other fields were required to expand the iron business. I had become interested, with my friends of the Pennsylvania Railroad Company, in building some railways in the Western States, but gradually withdrew from all such enterprises and made up my mind to go entirely contrary to the adage not to put all one's eggs in one basket. I determined that the proper policy was "to put all good eggs in one basket and then watch that basket."

I believe the true road to preëminent success in any line is to make yourself master in that line. I have no faith in the policy of scattering one's resources, and in my experience I have rarely if ever met a man who achieved preëminence in money-making—certainly never one in manufacturing—who was interested in many concerns. The men who have succeeded are men who have chosen one line and stuck to it. It is surprising how few men appreciate the enormous dividends derivable from investment in their own business. There is scarcely a manufacturer in the world who has not in his works some machinery that should be thrown out and replaced by improved appliances; or who does not for the want of additional machinery or new methods lose more than sufficient to pay the largest dividend obtainable by investment beyond his own domain. And yet most business men whom I have known invest in bank shares and in far-away enterprises, while the true gold mine lies right in their own factories.

I have tried always to hold fast to this important fact. It has been with me a cardinal doctrine that I could manage my own capital better than any other person, much better than any board of directors. The losses men encounter during a business life which seriously embarrass them are rarely in their own business, but in enterprises of which the investor is not master. My advice to young men would be not only to concentrate their whole time and attention on the one business in life in which they engage, but to put every dollar of their capital into it. If there be any business that will not bear extension, the true policy is to invest the surplus in first-class securities which will yield a moderate but certain revenue if some other growing business cannot be found. As for myself my decision was taken early. I would concentrate upon the manufacture of iron and steel and be master in that.

As we had been compelled to engage in the manufacture of wrought-iron in order to make bridges and other structures, so now we thought it desirable to manufacture our own pig iron. And this led to the erection of the Lucy Furnace in the year 1870—a venture which would have been postponed had we fully appreciated its magnitude. We heard from time to time the ominous predictions made by our older brethren in the manufacturing business with regard to the rapid growth and extension of our young concern, but we were not deterred. We thought we had sufficient capital and credit to justify the building of one blast furnace.

The estimates made of its cost, however, did not

cover more than half the expenditure. It was an experiment with us. Mr. Kloman knew nothing about blast-furnace operations. But even without exact knowledge no serious blunder was made. The yield of the Lucy Furnace (named after my bright sister-in-law) exceeded our most sanguine expectations and the then unprecedented output of a hundred tons per day was made from one blast furnace, for one week—an output that the world had never heard of before. We held the record and many visitors came to marvel at the marvel.

It was not, however, all smooth sailing with our iron business. Years of panic came at intervals. We had passed safely through the fall in values following the war, when iron from nine cents per pound dropped to three. Many failures occurred and our financial manager had his time fully occupied in providing funds to meet emergencies. Among many wrecks our firm stood with credit unimpaired. But the manufacture of pig iron gave us more anxiety than any other department of our business so far. The greatest service rendered us in this branch of manufacturing was by Mr. Whitwell, of the celebrated Whitwell Brothers of England, whose blast-furnace stoves were so generally used. Mr. Whitwell was one of the best-known of the visitors who came to marvel at the Lucy Furnace, and I laid the difficulty we then were experiencing before him. He said immediately:

"That comes from the angle of the bell being wrong."

He explained how it should be changed. Our Mr. Kloman was slow to believe this, but I urged that a small glass-model furnace and two bells be made, one as the Lucy was and the other as Mr. Whitwell advised it should be. This was done, and upon my next visit experiments were made with each, the result being just as Mr. Whitwell had foretold. Our bell distributed the large pieces to the sides of the furnace, leaving the center a dense mass through which the blast could only partially penetrate. The Whitwell bell threw the pieces to the center leaving the circumference dense. This made all the difference in the world. The Lucy's troubles were over.

What a kind, big, broad man was Mr. Whitwell, with no narrow jealousy, no withholding his knowledge! We had in some departments learned new things and were able to be of service to his firm in return. At all events, after that everything we had was open to the Whitwells.

CHAPTER XII

THE AGE OF STEEL

LOOKING back to-day it seems incredible that only forty years ago (1870) chemistry in the United States was an almost unknown agent in connection with the manufacture of pig iron. It was the agency, above all others, most needful in the manufacture of iron and steel. The blast-furnace manager of that day was usually a rude bully, generally a foreigner, who in addition to his other acquirements was able to knock down a man now and then as a lesson to the other unruly spirits under him. He was supposed to diagnose the condition of the furnace by instinct, to possess some almost supernatural power of divination, like his congener in the country districts who was reputed to be able to locate an oil well or water supply by means of a hazel rod. He was a veritable quack doctor who applied whatever remedies occurred to him for the troubles of his patient.

The Lucy Furnace was out of one trouble and into another, owing to the great variety of ores, limestone, and coke which were then supplied with little or no regard to their component parts. This state of affairs became intolerable to us. We finally decided to dispense with the rule-of-thumb-and-intuition manager, and to place a young man in charge of the furnace. We had a young shipping clerk, Henry M. Curry, who had distinguished himself, and it was resolved to make him manager.

Mr. Phipps had the Lucy Furnace under his special charge. His daily visits to it saved us from failure there. Not that the furnace was not doing as well as other furnaces in the West as to money-making, but being so much larger than other furnaces its variations entailed much more serious results.

The next step taken was to find a chemist as Mr. Curry's assistant and guide. We found the man in a learned German, Dr. Fricke, and great secrets did the doctor open up to us. Iron stone from mines that had a high reputation was now found to contain ten, fifteen, and even twenty per cent less iron than it had been credited with. Mines that hitherto had a poor reputation we found to be now yielding superior ore. The good was bad and the bad was good, and everything was topsy-turvy. Nine tenths of all the uncertainties of pig-iron making were dispelled under the burning sun of chemical knowledge.

At a most critical period when it was necessary for the credit of the firm that the blast furnace should make its best product, it had been stopped because an exceedingly rich and pure ore had been substituted for an inferior ore—an ore which did not yield more than two thirds of the quantity of iron of the other. The furnace had met with disaster because too much lime had been used to flux this exceptionally pure iron stone. The very superiority of the materials had involved us in serious losses.

What fools we had been! But then there was this consolation: we were not as great fools as our competitors. It was years after we had taken chemistry to guide us that it was said by the proprietors of some other furnaces that they could not afford to employ a chemist. Had they known the truth then, they would have known that they could not afford to be without one. Looking back it seems pardonable to record that we were the first to employ a chemist at blast furnaces —something our competitors pronounced extravagant.

The Lucy Furnace became the most profitable branch of our business, because we had almost the entire monopoly of scientific management. Having discovered the secret, it was not long (1872) before we decided to erect an additional furnace. This was done with great economy as compared with our first experiment. The mines which had no reputation and the products of which many firms would not permit to be used in their blast furnaces found a purchaser in us. Those mines which were able to obtain an enormous price for their products, owing to a reputation for quality, we quietly ignored. A curious illustration of this was the celebrated Pilot Knob mine in Missouri. Its product was, so to speak, under a cloud. A small portion of it only could be used, it was said, without obstructing the furnace. Chemistry told us that it was low in phosphorus, but very high in silicon. There was no better ore and scarcely any as rich, if it were properly fluxed. We therefore bought heavily of this and received the thanks of the proprietors for rendering their property valuable.

It is hardly believable that for several years we were able to dispose of the highly phosphoric cinder from the puddling furnaces at a higher price than we had to pay for the pure cinder from the heating furnaces of our competitors—a cinder which was richer in iron than the puddled cinder and much freer from phosphorus. Upon some occasion a blast furnace had attempted to smelt the flue cinder, and from its greater purity the furnace did not work well with a mixture intended for an impurer article; hence for years it was thrown over the banks of the river at Pittsburgh by our competitors as worthless. In some cases we were even able to exchange a poor article for a good one and obtain a bonus.

But it is still more unbelievable that a prejudice, equally unfounded, existed against putting into the blast furnaces the roll-scale from the mills which was pure oxide of iron. This reminds me of my dear friend and fellow-Dunfermline townsman, Mr. Chisholm, of Cleveland. We had many pranks together. One day, when I was visiting his works at Cleveland, I saw men wheeling this valuable roll-scale into the yard. I asked Mr. Chisholm where they were going with it, and he said:

"To throw it over the bank. Our managers have always complained that they had bad luck when they attempted to remelt it in the blast furnace."

I said nothing, but upon my return to Pittsburgh I set about having a joke at his expense. We had then a young man in our service named Du Puy, whose father was known as the inventor of a direct process in iron-making with which he was then experimenting in Pittsburgh. I recommended our people to send Du Puy to Cleveland to contract for all the roll-scale of my friend's establishment. He did so, buying it for fifty cents per ton and having it shipped to him direct. This continued for some time. I expected always to hear of the joke being discovered. The premature death of Mr. Chisholm occurred before I could apprise him of it. His successors soon, however, followed our example.

I had not failed to notice the growth of the Bessemer process. If this proved successful I knew that iron was destined to give place to steel; that the Iron Age would pass away and the Steel Age take its place. My friend,

John A. Wright, president of the Freedom Iron Works at Lewiston, Pennsylvania, had visited England purposely to investigate the new process. He was one of our best and most experienced manufacturers, and his decision was so strongly in its favor that he induced his company to erect Bessemer works. He was quite right, but just a little in advance of his time. The capital required was greater than he estimated. More than this, it was not to be expected that a process which was even then in somewhat of an experimental stage in Britain could be transplanted to the new country and operated successfully from the start. The experiment was certain to be long and costly, and for this my friend had not made sufficient allowance.

At a later date, when the process had become established in England, capitalists began to erect the present Pennsylvania Steel Works at Harrisburg. These also had to pass through an experimental stage and at a critical moment would probably have been wrecked but for the timely assistance of the Pennsylvania Railroad Company. It required a broad and able man like President Thomson, of the Pennsylvania Railroad, to recommend to his board of directors that so large a sum as six hundred thousand dollars should be advanced to a manufacturing concern on his road, that steel rails might be secured for the line. The result fully justified his action.

The question of a substitute for iron rails upon the Pennsylvania Railroad and other leading lines had become a very serious one. Upon certain curves at Pittsburgh, on the road connecting the Pennsylvania with the Fort Wayne, I had seen new iron rails placed every six weeks or two months. Before the Bessemer process was known I had called President Thomson's

Skibo Castle (see p. 129).

Andrew Carnegie, his wife and daughter.

attention to the efforts of Mr. Dodds in England, who had carbonized the heads of iron rails with good results. I went to England and obtained control of the Dodds patents and recommended President Thomson to appropriate twenty thousand dollars for experiments at Pittsburgh, which he did. We built a furnace on our grounds at the upper mill and treated several hundred tons of rails for the Pennsylvania Railroad Company and with remarkably good results as compared with iron rails. These were the first hard-headed rails used in America. We replaced them on some of the sharpest curves and their superior service far more than compensated for the advance made by Mr. Thomson. Had the Bessemer process not been successfully developed, I verily believe that we should ultimately have been able to improve the Dodds process sufficiently to make its adoption general. But there was nothing to be compared with the solid steel article which the Bessemer process produced.

Our friends of the Cambia Iron Company at Johnstown, near Pittsburgh—the principal manufacturers of rails in America—decided to erect a Bessemer plant. In England I had seen it demonstrated, at least to my satisfaction, that the process could be made a grand success without undue expenditure of capital or great risk. Mr. William Coleman, who was ever alive to new methods, arrived at the same conclusion. It was agreed we should enter upon the manufacture of steel rails at Pittsburgh. He became a partner and also my dear friend Mr. David McCandless, who had so kindly offered aid to my mother at my father's death. The latter was not forgotten. Mr. John Scott and Mr. David A. Stewart, and others joined me; Mr. Edgar Thomson and Mr. Thomas A. Scott, president and vice-president of the Pennsylvania Railroad, also became stockholders, anxious to encourage the development of steel. The steel-rail company was organized January 1, 1873.

The question of location was the first to engage our serious attention. I could not reconcile myself to any location that was proposed, and finally went to Pittsburgh to consult with my partners about it. The subject was constantly in my mind and in bed one morning the site suddenly appeared to me. I rose and called to my brother:

"Tom, you and Mr. Coleman are right about the location; right at Braddock's, between the Pennsylvania, the Baltimore and Ohio, and the river, is the best situation in America; and let's call the works after our dear friend Edgar Thomson. Let us go over to Mr. Coleman's and drive out to Braddock's."

We did so that day, and the next morning Mr. Coleman was at work trying to secure the property. Mr. McKinney, the owner, had a high idea of the value of his farm. What we had expected to purchase for five or six hundred dollars an acre cost us two thousand. But since then we have been compelled to add to our original purchase at a cost of five thousand dollars per acre.

There, on the very field of Braddock's defeat, we began the erection of our steel-rail mills. In excavating for the foundations many relics of the battle were found —bayonets, swords, and the like.

In naming the steel mills as we did the desire was to honor my friend Edgar Thomson, but when I asked permission to use his name his reply was significant. He said that as far as American steel rails were concerned, he did not feel that he wished to connect his name with them, for they had proved to be far from creditable. Uncertainty was, of course, inseparable from the experimental stage; but, when I assured him that it was now possible to make steel rails in America as good in every particular as the foreign article, and that we intended to obtain for our rails the reputation enjoyed by the Keystone bridges and the Kloman axles, he consented.

He was very anxious to have us purchase land upon the Pennsylvania Railroad, as his first thought was always for that company. This would have given the Pennsylvania a monopoly of our traffic. When he visited Pittsburgh a few months later and Mr. Robert Pitcairn, my successor as superintendent of the Pittsburgh Division of the Pennsylvania, pointed out to him the situation of the new works at Braddock's Station, which gave us not only a connection with his own line, but also with the rival Baltimore and Ohio line, and with a rival in one respect greater than either—the Ohio River—he said, with a twinkle of his eye to Robert, as Robert told me:

"Andy should have located his works a few miles farther east." But Mr. Thomson knew the good and sufficient reasons which determined the selection of the unrivaled site.

The works were well advanced when the financial panic of September, 1873, came upon us. I then entered upon the most anxious period of my business life. All was going well when one morning in our summer cottage, in the Allegheny Mountains at Cresson, a telegram came announcing the failure of Jay Cooke & Co. Almost every hour after brought news of some fresh disaster. House after house failed. The question every morning was which would go next. Every failure depleted the resources of other concerns.

Loss after loss ensued, until a total paralysis of business set in. Every weak spot was discovered and houses that otherwise would have been strong were borne down largely because our country lacked a proper banking system.

We had not much reason to be anxious about our debts. Not what we had to pay of our own debts could give us much trouble, but rather what we might have to pay for our debtors. It was not our bills payable but our bills receivable which required attention, for we soon had to begin meeting both. Even our own banks had to beg us not to draw upon our balances. One incident will shed some light upon the currency situation. One of our pay-days was approaching. One hundred thousand dollars in small notes were absolutely necessary, and to obtain these we paid a premium of twenty-four hundred dollars in New York and had them expressed to Pittsburgh. It was impossible to borrow money, even upon the best collaterals; but by selling securities, which I had in reserve, considerable sums were realized—the company undertaking to replace them later.

It happened that some of the railway companies whose lines centered in Pittsburgh owed us large sums for material furnished—the Fort Wayne road being the largest debtor. I remember calling upon Mr. Thaw, the vice-president of the Fort Wayne, and telling him we must have our money. He replied:

"You ought to have your money, but we are not paying anything these days that is not protestable."

"Very good," I said, "your freight bills are in that category and we shall follow your excellent example. Now I am going to order that we do not pay you one dollar for freight."

"Well, if you do that," he said, "we will stop your freight."

I said we would risk that. The railway company could not proceed to that extremity. And as a matter of fact we ran for some time without paying the freight bills. It was simply impossible for the manufacturers of Pittsburgh to pay their accruing liabilities when their customers stopped payment. The banks were forced to renew maturing paper. They behaved splendidly to us, as they always have done, and we steered safely through. But in a critical period like this there was one thought uppermost with me, to gather more capital and keep it in our business so that come what would we should never again be called upon to endure such nights and days of racking anxiety.

Speaking for myself in this great crisis, I was at first the most excited and anxious of the partners. I could scarcely control myself. But when I finally saw the strength of our financial position I became philosophically cool and found myself quite prepared, if necessary, to enter the directors' rooms of the various banks with which we dealt, and lay our entire position before their boards. I felt that this could result in nothing discreditable to us. No one interested in our business had lived extravagantly. Our manner of life had been the very reverse of this. No money had been withdrawn from the business to build costly homes, and, above all, not one of us had made speculative ventures upon the stock exchange, or invested in any other enterprises than those connected with the main business. Neither had we exchanged endorsements with others. Besides this we could show a prosperous business that was making money every year.

I was thus enabled to laugh away the fears of my

partners, but none of them rejoiced more than I did that the necessity for opening our lips to anybody about our finances did not arise.

When the cyclone of 1873 struck us we at once began to reef sail in every quarter. Very reluctantly did we decide that the construction of the new steel works must cease for a time. Several prominent persons, who had invested in them, became unable to meet their payments and I was compelled to take over their interests, repaying the full cost to all. In that way control of the company came into my hands.

Up to this time I had the reputation in business of being a bold, fearless, and perhaps a somewhat reckless young man. Our operations had been extensive, our growth rapid and, although still young, I had been handling millions. My own career was thought by the elderly ones of Pittsburgh to have been rather more brilliant than substantial. I know of an experienced one who declared that if "Andrew Carnegie's brains did not carry him through his luck would." But I think nothing could be farther from the truth than the estimate thus suggested. I am sure that any competent judge would be surprised to find how little I ever risked for myself or my partners. When I did big things, some large corporation like the Pennsylvania Railroad Company was behind me and the responsible party. My supply of Scotch caution never has been small; but I was apparently something of a dare-devil now and then to the manufacturing fathers of Pittsburgh. They were old and I was young, which made all the difference.

The fright which Pittsburgh financial institutions had with regard to myself and our enterprises rapidly gave place to perhaps somewhat unreasoning confidence. Our credit became unassailable, and thereafter in times of financial pressure the offerings of money to us increased rather than diminished, just as the deposits of the old Bank of Pittsburgh were never so great as when the deposits in other banks ran low. It was the only bank in America which redeemed its circulation in gold, disdaining to take refuge under the law and pay its obligations in greenbacks. It had few notes, and I doubt not the decision paid as an advertisement.

In addition to the embarrassment of my friends Mr. Scott, Mr. Thomson, and others, there came upon us later an even severer trial in the discovery that our partner, Mr. Andrew Kloman, had been led by a party of speculative people into the Escanaba Iron Company. He was assured that the concern was to be made a stock company, but before this was done his colleagues had succeeded in creating an enormous amount of liabilities —about seven hundred thousand dollars. There was nothing but bankruptcy as a means of reinstating Mr. Kloman.

This gave us more of a shock than all that had preceded, because Mr. Kloman, being a partner, had no right to invest in another iron company, or in any other company involving personal debt, without informing his partners. There is one imperative rule for men in business—no secrets from partners. Disregard of this rule involved not only Mr. Kloman himself, but our company, in peril. The question for a time was whether there was anything really sound. Where could we find bedrock upon which we could stand?

Had Mr. Kloman been a business man it would have been impossible ever to allow him to be a partner with us again after this discovery. He was not such, however, but the ablest of practical mechanics with some business ability. Mr. Kloman's ambition had been to be in the office, where he was worse than useless, rather than in the mill devising and running new machinery, where he was without a peer. We had some difficulty in placing him in his proper position and keeping him there, which may have led him to seek an outlet elsewhere. He was perhaps flattered by men who were well known in the community; and in this case he was led by persons who knew how to reach him by extolling his wonderful business abilities in addition to his mechanical genius —abilities which his own partners, as already suggested, but faintly recognized.

After Mr. Kloman had passed through the bankruptcy court and was again free, we offered him a ten per cent interest in our business, charging for it only the actual capital invested, with nothing whatever for good-will. This we were to carry for him until the profits paid for it. We were to charge interest only on the cost, and he was to assume no responsibility. The offer was accompanied by the condition that he should not enter into any other business or endorse for others, but give his whole time and attention to the mechanical and not the business management of the mills. Could he have been persuaded to accept this, he would have been a multimillionaire; but his pride, and more particularly that of his family, perhaps, would not permit this. He would go into business on his own account, and, notwithstanding the most urgent appeals on my part, and that of my colleagues, he persisted in the determination to start a new rival concern with his sons as business managers. The result was failure and premature death.

How foolish we are not to recognize what we are best fitted for and can perform, not only with ease but with pleasure, as masters of the craft. More than one able man I have known has persisted in blundering in an office when he had great talent for the mill, and has worn himself out, oppressed with cares and anxieties, his life a continual round of misery, and the result at last failure. I never regretted parting with any man so much as Mr. Kloman. His was a good heart, a great mechanical brain, and had he been left to himself I believe he would have been glad to remain with us. Offers of capital from others—offers which failed when needed—turned his head, and the great mechanic soon proved the poor man of affairs.

CHAPTER XIII

PARTNERS, BOOKS, AND TRAVEL

WHEN Mr. Kloman had severed his connection with us there was no hesitation in placing William Borntraeger in charge of the mills. It has always been with especial pleasure that I have pointed to the career of William. He came direct from Germany—a young man who could not speak English, but being distantly connected with Mr. Kloman was employed in the mills, at first in a minor capacity. He promptly learned English and became a shipping clerk at six dollars per week. He had not a particle of mechanical knowledge, and yet such was his unflagging zeal and industry for the interests of his employer that he soon became marked for being everywhere about the mill, knowing everything, and attending to everything.

William was a character. He never got over his German idioms and his inverted English made his remarks very effective. Under his superintendence the Union Iron Mills became a most profitable branch of our business. He had overworked himself after a few years' application and we decided to give him a trip to Europe. He came to New York by way of Washington. When he called upon me in New York he expressed himself as more anxious to return to Pittsburgh than to revisit Germany. In ascending the Washington Monument he had seen the Carnegie beams in the stairway and also at other points in public buildings, and as he expressed it:

"It yust make me so broud dat I want to go right back and see dat everyting is going right at de mill."

Early hours in the morning and late in the dark hours at night William was in the mills. His life was there. He was among the first of the young men we admitted to partnership, and the poor German lad at his death was in receipt of an income, as I remember, of about $50,000 a year, every cent of which was deserved. Stories about him are many.

Captain Evans ("Fighting Bob") was at one time government inspector at our mills. He was a severe one. William was sorely troubled at times and finally offended the Captain, who complained of his behavior. We tried to get William to realize the importance of pleasing a government official. William's reply was:

"But he gomes in and smokes my cigars" (bold Captain! William reveled in one-cent Wheeling tobies) "and then he goes and contems my iron. What does you tinks of a man like dat? But I apologize and dreat him right to-morrow."

The Captain was assured William had agreed to make due amends, but he laughingly told us afterward that William's apology was:

"Vell, Captain, I hope you vas all right dis morning. I haf noting against you, Captain," holding out his hand, which the Captain finally took and all was well.

William once sold to our neighbor, the pioneer steel-maker of Pittsburgh, James Park, a large lot of old rails which we could not use. Mr. Park found them of a very bad quality. He made claims for damages and William was told that he must go with Mr. Phipps to meet Mr. Park and settle. Mr. Phipps went into Mr. Park's office, while William took a look around the works in search of the condemned material, which was nowhere to be seen. Well did William know where to look. He finally entered the office, and before Mr. Park had time to say a word William began:

"Mr. Park, I vas glad to hear dat de old rails what I sell you don't suit for steel. I will buy dem all from you back, five dollars ton profit for you." Well did William know that they had all been used. Mr. Park was nonplussed, and the affair ended. William had triumphed.

Upon one of my visits to Pittsburgh William told me he had something "particular" he wished to tell me—something he couldn't tell any one else. This was upon his return from the trip to Germany. There he had been asked to visit for a few days a former schoolfellow, who had risen to be a professor:

"Well, Mr. Carnegie, his sister who kept his house was very kind to me, and ven I got to Hamburg I tought I sent her yust a little present. She write me a letter, then I write her a letter. She write me and I write her, and den I ask her would she marry me. She was very educated, but she write yes. Den I ask her to come to New York, and I meet her dere, but, Mr. Carnegie, dem people don't know noting about business and de mills. Her bruder write me dey want me to go dere again and marry her in Chairmany, and I can go away not again from de mills. I tought I yust ask you aboud it."

"Of course you can go again. Quite right, William, you should go. I think the better of her people for feeling so. You go over at once and bring her home. I'll arrange it." Then, parting, I said: "William, I suppose your sweetheart is a beautiful, tall, 'peaches-and-cream' kind of German young lady."

"Vell, Mr. Carnegie, she is a leetle stout. If *I had*

the rolling of her I give her yust one more pass." All William's illustrations were founded on mill practice.

Mr. Curry had distinguished himself by this time in his management of the Lucy Furnaces, and he took his place among the partners, sharing equally with the others. There is no way of making a business successful that can vie with the policy of promoting those who render exceptional service. We finally converted the firm of Carnegie, McCandless & Co. into the Edgar Thomson Steel Company, and included my brother and Mr. Phipps, both of whom had declined at first to go into the steel business with their too enterprising senior. But when I showed them the earnings for the first year and told them if they did not get into steel they would find themselves in the wrong boat, they both reconsidered and came with us. It was fortunate for them as for us.

In 1874 the mills were at last about ready to begin and an organization the auditor proposed was laid before me for approval. I found he had divided the works into two departments and had given control of one to Mr. Stevenson, a Scotsman who afterwards made a fine record as a manufacturer, and control of the other to a Mr. Jones. Nothing, I am certain, ever affected the success of the steel company more than the decision which I gave upon that proposal. Upon no account could two men be in the same works with equal authority. An army with two commanders-in-chief, a ship with two captains, could not fare more disastrously than a manufacturing concern with two men in command upon the same ground, even though in two different departments. I said:

"This will not do. I do not know Mr. Stevenson, nor do I know Mr. Jones, but one or the other must be made captain and he alone must report to you."

The decision fell upon Mr. Jones and in this way we obtained "The Captain," who afterward made his name famous wherever the manufacture of Bessemer steel is known.

The Captain was then quite young, spare and active, bearing traces of his Welsh descent even in his stature, for he was quite short. He came to us as a two-dollar-a-day mechanic from the neighboring works at Johnstown. We soon saw that he was a character. Every movement told it. He had volunteered as a private during the Civil War and carried himself so finely that he became captain of a company which was never known to flinch. Much of the success of the Edgar Thomson Works belongs to this man.

In later years he declined an interest in the firm which would have made him a millionaire. I told him one day that some of the young men who had been given an interest were now making much more than he was and we had voted to make him a partner. This entailed no financial responsibility, as we always provided that the cost of the interest given was payable only out of profits.

"No," he said, "I don't want to have my thoughts running on business. I have enough trouble looking after these works. Just give me a thumping big salary if you think I'm worth it."

"All right, Captain, the salary of the President of the United States is yours."

"That's the talk," said the little Welshman.[1]

[1] The story is told that when Mr. Carnegie was selecting his younger partners he one day sent for a young Scotsman, Alexander R. Peacock, and asked him rather abruptly:

"Peacock, what would you give to be made a millionaire?"

"A liberal discount for cash, sir," was the answer.

He was a partner owning a two per cent interest when the Carnegie Steel Company was merged into the United States Steel Corporation.

Our competitors in steel were at first disposed to ignore us. Knowing the difficulties they had in starting their own steel works, they could not believe we would be ready to deliver rails for another year and declined to recognize us as competitors. The price of steel rails when we began was about seventy dollars per ton. We sent our agent through the country with instructions to take orders at the best prices he could obtain; and before our competitors knew it, we had obtained a large number—quite sufficient to justify us in making a start.

So perfect was the machinery, so admirable the plans, so skillful were the men selected by Captain Jones, and so great a manager was he himself, that our success was phenomenal. I think I place a unique statement on record when I say that the result of the first month's operations left a margin of profit of $11,000. It is also remarkable that so perfect was our system of accounts that we knew the exact amount of the profit. We had learned from experience in our iron works what exact accounting meant. There is nothing more profitable than clerks to check up each transfer of material from one department to another in process of manufacture.

The new venture in steel having started off so promisingly, I began to think of taking a holiday, and my long-cherished purpose of going around the world came to the front. Mr. J. W. Vandevort ("Vandy") and I accordingly set out in the autumn of 1878. I took with me several pads suitable for penciling and began to make a few notes day by day, not with any intention of publishing a book; but thinking, perhaps, I might print a few copies of my notes for private circulation. The sensation which one has when he first sees his remarks in the form of a printed book is great. When the package came from the printers I re-read the book trying to decide whether it was worth while to send copies to my friends. I came to the conclusion that upon the whole it was best to do so and await the verdict.

The responses in my case exceeded expectations, and were of such a character as to satisfy me that the writers really had enjoyed the book, or meant at least a part of what they said about it. Every author is prone to believe sweet words. Among the first that came were in a letter from Anthony Drexel, Philadelphia's great banker, complaining that I had robbed him of several hours of sleep. Having begun the book he could not lay it down and retired at two o'clock in the morning after finishing. Several similar letters were received. I remember Mr. Huntington, president of the Central Pacific Railway, meeting me one morning and saying he was going to pay me a great compliment.

"What is it?" I asked.

"Oh, I read your book from end to end."

"Well," I said, "that is not such a great compliment. Others of our mutual friends have done that."

"Oh, yes, but probably none of your friends are like me. I have not read a book for years except my ledger and I did not intend to read yours, but when I began it I could not lay it down. My ledger is the only book I have gone through for five years."

I was not disposed to credit all that my friends said, but others who had obtained the book from them were pleased with it and I lived for some months under intoxicating, but I trust not perilously pernicious, flattery. Several editions of the book were printed to meet the request for copies. Some notices of it and extracts got into the papers, and finally Charles

Carnegie Library, Dunfermline — the first of almost 3,000 donated by Andrew Carnegie (see p. 135).

Roll of Honour of the Carnegie Hero Fund Trust — on display at the Andrew Carnegie Birthplace Museum, Dunfermline (see p. 139).

Scribner's Sons asked to publish it for the market. So *Round the World* came before the public and I was at last "an author."

A new horizon was opened up to me by this voyage.

Every person who can, even at a sacrifice, make the voyage around the world should do so. All other travel compared to it seems incomplete, gives us merely vague impressions of parts of the whole. When the circle has been completed, you feel on your return that you have seen (of course only in the mass) all there is to be seen. The parts fit into one symmetrical whole and you see humanity wherever it is placed working out a destiny tending to one definite end.

The conclusion reached will be that the inhabitants of each country rejoice that their lot has been cast where it is, and are disposed to pity the less fortunate condemned to live beyond their sacred limits. The masses of all nations are usually happy, each mass certain that:

"East or West
Home is best."

Two illustrations of this from our *Round the World* trip may be noted:

"Visiting the tapioca workers in the woods near Singapore, we found them busily engaged, the children running about stark naked, the parents clothed in the usual loose rags. Our party attracted great attention. We asked our guide to tell the people that we came from a country where the water in such a pond as that before us would become solid at this season of the year and we could walk upon it and that sometimes it would be so hard horses and wagons crossed wide rivers on the ice. They wondered and asked why we didn't come and live among them. They really were very happy."

Again:

"On the way to the North Cape we visited a reindeer camp of the Laplanders. A sailor from the ship was deputed to go with the party. I walked homeward with him, and as we approached the fiord looking down and over to the opposite shore we saw a few straggling huts and one two-story house under construction. What is that new building for? we asked.

"'That is to be the home of a man born in Tromso who has made a great deal of money and has now come back to spend his days there. He is very rich.'

"'You told me you had traveled all over the world. You have seen London, New York, Calcutta, Melbourne, and other places. If you made a fortune like that man what place would you make your home in old age?' His eye glistened as he said:

"'Ah, there's no place like Tromso.' This is in the Arctic Circle, six months of night, but he had been born in Tromso. Home, sweet, sweet home!"

CHAPTER XIV

THE MAN WHO WAS TOO RICH

THE Freedom of my native town (Dunfermline) was conferred upon me July 12, 1877, the first Freedom and the greatest honor I ever received. I was overwhelmed. Only two signatures upon the roll came between mine and Sir Walter Scott's, who had been made a Burgess. My parents had seen him one day sketching Dunfermline Abbey and often told me about his appearance. My speech in reply to the Freedom was the subject of much concern. I spoke to my Uncle Bailie Morrison, telling him I just felt like saying so and so, as this really was in my heart. He was an orator himself and he spoke words of wisdom to me then.

"Just say that, Andra; nothing like saying just what you really feel."

It was a lesson in public speaking which I took to heart. There is one rule I might suggest for youthful orators. When you stand up before an audience reflect that there are before you only men and women. You should speak to them as you speak to other men and women in daily intercourse. If you are not trying to be something different from yourself, there is no more occasion for embarrassment than if you were talking in your office to a party of your own people—none whatever. It is trying to be other than one's self that unmans one. Be your own natural self and go ahead.

I spoke again at Dunfermline, July 27, 1881, when my mother laid the foundation stone there of the first free library building I ever gave. My father was one of five weavers who founded the earliest library in the town by opening their own books to their neighbors. Dunfermline named the building I gave "Carnegie Library." The architect asked for my coat of arms. I informed him I had none, but suggested that above the door there might be carved a rising sun shedding its rays with the motto: "Let there be light." This he adopted.

We had come up to Dunfermline with a coaching party. When walking through England in the year 1867 with George Lauder and Harry Phipps I had formed the idea of coaching from Brighton to Inverness with a party of my dearest friends. The time had come for the long-promised trip, and in the spring of 1881 we sailed from New York, a party of eleven, to enjoy one of the happiest excursions of my life. It was one of the holidays from business that kept me young and happy—worth all the medicine in the world.

All the notes I made of the coaching trip were a few lines a day in twopenny pass-books bought before we started. As with *Round the World*, I thought that I might some day write a magazine article, or give some account of my excursion for those who accompanied me; but one wintry day I decided that it was scarcely worth while to go down to the New York office, three miles distant, and the question was how I should occupy the spare time. I thought of the coaching trip, and decided to write a few lines just to see how I should get on. The narrative flowed freely, and before the day was over I had written between three and four thousand words. I took up the pleasing task every stormy day when it was unnecessary for me to visit the office, and in exactly twenty sittings I had finished a book. I handed the notes to Scribner's people and asked them to print a few hundred copies for private circulation. The volume pleased my friends, as *Round the World* had done. Mr. Champlin one day told me that Mr. Scribner had read the book and would like very much to publish it for general circulation upon his own account, subject to a royalty, and I consented. Any merit that the book has comes, I am sure, from the total absence of effort on my part to make an impression. I wrote for my friends; and what one does easily, one does well. I reveled in the writing of the book, as I had in the journey itself.

The year 1886 ended in deep gloom for me. My life as a happy careless young man, with every want looked after, was over. I was left alone in the world. My mother and brother passed away in November, within a few days of each other, while I lay in bed under a severe attack of typhoid fever, unable to move and, perhaps fortunately, unable to feel the full weight of the catastrophe, being myself face to face with death.

I was the first stricken, upon returning from a visit in the East to our Cottage at Cresson Springs on top of the Alleghenies where my mother and I spent our happy summers. I had been quite unwell for a day or two before leaving New York. A physician being summoned, my trouble was pronounced typhoid fever. Professor Dennis was called from New York and he corroborated the diagnosis. An attendant physician and trained nurse were provided at once. Soon after my mother broke down and my brother in Pittsburgh also was reported ill.

I was despaired of, I was so low, and then my whole nature seemed to change. I became reconciled, indulged in pleasing meditations, was without the slightest pain.

My mother's and brother's serious condition had not been revealed to me, and when I was informed that both had left me forever it seemed only natural that I should follow them. We had never been separated; why should we be now? But it was decreed otherwise.

I recovered slowly and the future began to occupy my thoughts. There was only one ray of hope and comfort in it. Toward that my thoughts always turned. For several years I had known Miss Louise Whitfield. Her mother permitted her to ride with me in the Central Park. We were both very fond of riding. Other young ladies were on my list. I had fine horses and often rode in the Park and around New York with one or the other of the circle. In the end the others all faded into ordinary beings. Miss Whitfield remained alone as the perfect one beyond any I had met.

My advances met with indifferent success. She was not without other and younger admirers. My wealth and future plans were against me. I was rich and had everything and she felt she could be of little use or benefit to me. Her ideal was to be the real helpmeet of a young, struggling man to whom she could and would be indispensable, as her mother had been to her father. The care of her own family had largely fallen upon her after her father's death when she was twenty-one. She was now twenty-eight; her views of life were formed. At times she seemed more favorable and we corresponded. Once, however, she returned my letters saying she felt she must put aside all thought of accepting me.

Professor and Mrs. Dennis took me from Cresson to their own home in New York, as soon as I could be removed, and I lay there some time under the former's personal supervision. Miss Whitfield called to see me, for I had written her the first words from Cresson I was able to write. She saw now that I needed her. I was left alone in the world. Now she could be in every sense the "helpmeet." Both her heart and head were now willing and the day was fixed. We were married in New York, April 22, 1887, and sailed for our honeymoon, which was passed on the Isle of Wight.

Her delight was intense in finding the wild flowers. She had read of Wandering Willie, Heartsease, Forget-me-nots, the Primrose, Wild Thyme, and the whole list of homely names that had been to her only names till now. Everything charmed her. Uncle Lauder and one of my cousins came down from Scotland and visited us, and then we soon followed to the residence at Kilgraston they had selected for us in which to spend the summer. Scotland captured her. There was no doubt about that. Her girlish reading had been of Scotland—Scott's novels and *Scottish Chiefs* being her favorites. She soon became more Scotch than I. All this was fulfilling my fondest dreams.

We spent some days in Dunfermline and enjoyed them much. The haunts and incidents of my boyhood were visited and recited to her by all and sundry. She got nothing but flattering accounts of her husband which gave me a good start with her.

I was presented with the Freedom of Edinburgh as we passed northward—Lord Rosebery making the speech. The crowd in Edinburgh was great. I addressed the working-men in the largest hall and received a present from them as did Mrs. Carnegie also—a brooch she values highly. She heard and saw the pipers in all their glory and begged there should be one at our home—a piper to walk around and waken us in the morning and also to play us in to dinner. American as she is to the core, and Connecticut Puritan at that, she declared that if condemned to live upon a lonely island and allowed to choose only one musical instrument, it would be the pipes. The piper was secured quickly enough. One called and presented credentials from Cluny McPherson. We engaged him and were preceded by him playing the pipes as we entered our Kilgraston house.

We enjoyed Kilgraston, although Mrs. Carnegie still longed for a wilder and more Highland home. Matthew Arnold visited us, as did Mr. and Mrs. Blaine, Senator and Mrs. Eugene Hale, and many friends. Mrs. Carnegie would have my relatives up from Dunfermline, especially the older uncles and aunties. She charmed every one. They expressed their surprise to me that she ever married me, but I told them I was equally surprised. The match had evidently been predestined.

The next year we were offered and took Cluny Castle. Our piper was just the man to tell us all about it. He had been born and bred there and perhaps influenced our selection of that residence where we spent several summers.

On March 30, 1897, there came to us our daughter. As I first gazed upon her Mrs. Carnegie said:

"Her name is Margaret after your mother. Now one request I have to make."

"What is it, Lou?"

"We must get a summer home since this little one has been given us. We cannot rent one and be obliged to go in and go out at a certain date. It should be our home."

"Yes," I agreed.

"I make only one condition."

"What is that?" I asked.

"It must be in the Highlands of Scotland."

"Bless you," was my reply. "That suits me. You know I have to keep out of the sun's rays, and where can we do that so surely as among the heather? I'll be a committee of one to inquire and report."

Skibo Castle was the result.

It is now twenty years since Mrs. Carnegie entered and changed my life, a few months after the passing of my mother and only brother left me alone in the world. My life has been made so happy by her that I cannot imagine myself living without her guardianship. I thought I knew her, but it was only the surface of her qualities I had seen and felt. Of their purity, holiness, wisdom, I had not sounded the depth. In every emergency of our active, changing, and in later years somewhat public life, in all her relations with others, including my family and her own, she has proved the diplomat and peace-maker. Peace and good-will attend her footsteps wherever her blessed influence extends. In the rare instances demanding heroic action it is she who first realizes this and plays the part.

The Peace-Maker has never had a quarrel in all her life, not even with a schoolmate, and there does not live a soul upon the earth who has met her who has the slightest cause to complain of neglect. Not that she does not welcome the best and gently avoid the undesirable—none is more fastidious than she—but neither rank, wealth, nor social position affects her one iota. She is incapable of acting or speaking rudely; all is in perfect good taste. Still, she never lowers the standard. Her intimates are only of the best. She is always thinking how she can do good to those around her—planning for this one and that in case of need and making such judicious arrangements or presents as surprise those coöperating with her.

I cannot imagine myself going through these twenty years without her. Nor can I endure the thought of living after her. In the course of nature I have not that to meet; but then the thought of what will be cast upon her, a woman left alone with so much requiring attention and needing a man to decide, gives me intense pain and I sometimes wish I had this to endure for her. But then she will have our blessed daughter in her life and perhaps that will keep her patient. Besides, Margaret needs her more than she does her father.

CHAPTER XV

HARD WORK BEGINS

AFTER my book, *The Gospel of Wealth*, was published, it was inevitable that I should live up to its teachings by ceasing to struggle for more wealth. I resolved to stop accumulating and begin the infinitely more serious and difficult task of wise distribution. Our profits had reached forty millions of dollars per year and the prospect of increased earnings before us was amazing. Our successors, the United States Steel Corporation, soon after the purchase, netted sixty millions in one year. Had our company continued in business and adhered to our plans of extension, we figured that seventy millions in that year might have been earned.

Steel had ascended the throne and was driving away all inferior material. It was clearly seen that there was a great future ahead; but so far as I was concerned I knew the task of distribution before me would tax me in my old age to the utmost.

At this juncture—that is, March, 1901—Mr. Schwab told me Mr. Morgan had said to him he should really like to know if I wished to retire from business; if so he thought he could arrange it. He also said he had consulted our partners and that they were disposed to sell, being attracted by the terms Mr. Morgan had offered. I told Mr. Schwab that if my partners were desirous to sell I would concur, and we finally sold.

There had been so much deception by speculators buying old iron and steel mills and foisting them upon innocent purchasers at inflated values—hundred-dollar shares in some cases selling for a trifle—that I declined to take anything for the common stock. Had I done so, it would have given me just about one hundred millions more of five per cent bonds, which Mr. Morgan said afterwards I could have obtained. Such was the prosperity and such the money value of our steel business. Events proved I should have been quite justified in asking the additional sum named, for the common stock has paid five per cent continuously since. But I had enough, as has been proved, to keep me busier than ever before, trying to distribute it.

My first distribution was to the men in the mills. The following letters and papers will explain the gift:

NEW YORK, N.Y., *March* 12, 1901

I make this first use of surplus wealth, four millions of first mortgage 5 per cent bonds, upon retiring from business, as an acknowledgment of the deep debt which I owe to the workmen who have contributed so greatly to my success. It is designed to relieve those who may suffer from accidents, and provide small pensions for those needing help in old age.

In addition I give one million dollars of such bonds, the proceeds thereof to be used to maintain the libraries and halls I have built for our workmen.

In return, the Homestead workmen presented the following address:

MUNHALL, PA., *Feb'y* 23, 1903

MR. ANDREW CARNEGIE
New York, N.Y.

DEAR SIR:

We, the employees of the Homestead Steel Works, desire by this means to express to you through our

Committee our great appreciation of your benevolence in establishing the "Andrew Carnegie Relief Fund," the first annual report of its operation having been placed before us during the past month.

The interest which you have always shown in your workmen has won for you an appreciation which cannot be expressed by mere words. Of the many channels through which you have sought to do good, we believe that the "Andrew Carnegie Relief Fund" stands first. We have personal knowledge of cares lightened and of hope and strength renewed in homes where human prospects seemed dark and discouraging.

Respectfully yours

Committee:
- HARRY F. ROSE, *Roller*
- JOHN BELL, JR., *Blacksmith*
- J. A. HORTON, *Timekeeper*
- WALTER A. GREIG, *Electric Foreman*
- HARRY CUSACK, *Yardmaster*

The Lucy Furnace men presented me with a beautiful silver plate and inscribed upon it the following address:

ANDREW CARNEGIE RELIEF FUND
LUCY FURNACES

Whereas, Mr. Andrew Carnegie, in his munificent philanthropy, has endowed the "Andrew Carnegie Relief Fund" for the benefit of employees of the Carnegie Company, Therefore be it

Resolved, that the employees of the Lucy Furnaces, in special meeting assembled, do convey to Mr. Andrew Carnegie their sincere thanks for an appreciation of his unexcelled and bounteous endowment, and furthermore be it

Resolved, that it is their earnest wish and prayer that his life may be long spared to enjoy the fruits of his works.

Committee:
- JAMES SCOTT, *Chairman*
- LOUIS A. HUTCHISON, *Secretary*
- JAMES DALY
- R. C. TAYLOR
- JOHN V. WARD
- FREDERICK VOELKER
- JOHN M. VEIGH

I sailed soon for Europe, and as usual some of my partners did not fail to accompany me to the steamer and bade me good-bye. But, oh! the difference to me! Say what we would, do what we would, the solemn change had come. This I could not fail to realize. The wrench was indeed severe and there was pain in the good-bye which was also a farewell.

Upon my return to New York some months later, I felt myself entirely out of place, but was much cheered by seeing several of "the boys" on the pier to welcome me—the same dear friends, but so different. I had lost my partners, but not my friends. This was something; it was much. Still a vacancy was left. I had now to take up my self-appointed task of wisely disposing of surplus wealth. That would keep me deeply interested.

One day my eyes happened to see a line in that most valuable paper, the *Scottish American*, in which I had found many gems. This was the line:

"The gods send thread for a web begun."

It seemed almost as if it had been sent directly to me. This sank into my heart, and I resolved to begin at once my first web. True enough, the gods sent thread in the proper form. Dr. J. S. Billings, of the New York Public Libraries, came as their agent, and of dollars, five and a quarter millions went at one stroke for sixty-eight branch libraries, promised for New York City. Twenty more libraries for Brooklyn followed.

My father, as I have stated, had been one of the five pioneers in Dunfermline who combined and gave access to their few books to their less fortunate neighbors. I had followed in his footsteps by giving my native town a library—its foundation stone laid by my mother—so that this public library was really my first gift. It was followed by giving a public library and hall to Allegheny City—our first home in America. President Harrison kindly accompanied me from Washington and opened these buildings. Soon after this, Pittsburgh asked for a library, which was given. This developed, in due course, into a group of buildings embracing a museum, a picture gallery, technical schools, and the Margaret Morrison School for Young Women. This group of buildings I opened to the public November 5, 1895. In Pittsburgh I had made my fortune and in the twenty-four millions already spent on this group, she gets back only a small part of what she gave, and to which she is richly entitled.

The second large gift was to found the Carnegie Institution of Washington. The 28th of January, 1902, I gave ten million dollars in five per cent bonds, to which there has been added sufficient to make the total cash value twenty-five millions of dollars, the additions being made upon record of results obtained.

When I showed President Roosevelt the list of the distinguished men who had agreed to serve as directors, he remarked: "You could not duplicate it." He strongly favored the foundation, which was incorporated by an act of Congress, April 28, 1904, as follows:

"To encourage in the broadest and most liberal manner investigations, research and discovery, and the application of knowledge to the improvement of mankind; and, in particular, to conduct, endow and assist investigation in any department of science, literature or art, and to this end to coöperate with governments, universities, colleges, technical schools, learned societies, and individuals."

The history of the achievements of this Institution is so well known through its publications that details here are unnecessary. I may, however, refer to two of its undertakings that are somewhat unique. It is doing a world-wide service with the wood-and-bronze yacht, *Carnegie*, which is voyaging around the world correcting the errors of the earlier surveys. Many of these ocean surveys have been found misleading, owing to variations of the compass. Bronze being non-magnetic, while iron and steel are highly so, previous observations have proved liable to error. A notable instance is that of the stranding of a Cunard steamship near the Azores. Captain Peters, of the *Carnegie*, thought it advisable to test this case and found that the captain of the ill-fated steamer was sailing on the course laid down upon the admiralty map, and was not to blame. The original observation was wrong. The error caused by variation was promptly corrected.

This is only one of numerous corrections reported to the nations who go down to the sea in ships. Their thanks are our ample reward. In the deed of gift I expressed the hope that our young Republic might some day be able to repay, at least in some degree, the great debt it owes to the older lands. Nothing gives me

The Palace of Peace, The Hague (see p. 146).

Portrait by Howard Russell Butler.

deeper satisfaction than the knowledge that it has to some extent already begun to do so.

With the unique service rendered by the wandering *Carnegie*, we may rank that of the fixed observatory upon Mount Wilson, California, at an altitude of 5886 feet. Professor Hale is in charge of it. He attended the gathering of leading astronomers in Rome one year, and such were his revelations there that these savants resolved their next meeting should be on top of Mount Wilson. And so it was.

There is but one Mount Wilson. From a depth seventy-two feet down in the earth photographs have been taken of new stars. On the first of these plates many new worlds—I believe sixteen—were discovered. On the second I think it was sixty new worlds which had come into our ken, and on the third plate there were estimated to be more than a hundred—several of them said to be twenty times the size of our sun. Some of them were so distant as to require eight years for their light to reach us, which inclines us to bow our heads whispering to ourselves, "All we know is as nothing to the unknown." When the monster new glass, three times larger than any existing, is in operation, what revelations are to come! I am assured if a race inhabits the moon they will be clearly seen.

The third delightful task was founding the Hero Fund, in which my whole heart was concerned. I had heard of a serious accident in a coal pit near Pittsburgh, and how the former superintendent, Mr. Taylor, although then engaged in other pursuits, had instantly driven to the scene, hoping to be of use in the crisis. Rallying volunteers, who responded eagerly, he led them down the pit to rescue those below. Alas, alas, he the heroic leader lost his own life.

I could not get the thought of this out of my mind. My dear, dear friend, Mr. Richard Watson Gilder, had sent me the following true and beautiful poem, and I re-read it the morning after the accident, and resolved then to establish the Hero Fund:

IN THE TIME OF PEACE

'Twas said: "When roll of drum and battle's roar
Shall cease upon the earth, O, then no more

The deed—the race—of heroes in the land."
But scarce that word was breathed when one small hand

Lifted victorious o'er a giant wrong
That had its victims crushed through ages long;

Some woman set her pale and quivering face
Firm as a rock against a man's disgrace;

A little child suffered in silence lest
His savage pain should wound a mother's breast;

Some quiet scholar flung his gauntlet down
And risked, in Truth's great name, the synod's frown;

A civic hero, in the calm realm of laws,
Did that which suddenly drew a world's applause;

And one to the pest his lithe young body gave
That he a thousand thousand lives might save.

Hence arose the five-million-dollar fund to reward heroes, or to support the families of heroes who perish in the effort to serve or save their fellows, and to supplement what employers or others do in contributing to the support of the families of those left destitute through accidents. This fund, established April 15, 1904, has proved from every point of view a decided success. I cherish a fatherly regard for it since no one suggested it to me. As far as I know, it never had been thought of; hence it is emphatically "my ain bairn." Later I extended it to my native land, Great Britain, with headquarters at Dunfermline—the Trustees of the Carnegie Dunfermline Trust undertaking its administration, and splendidly have they succeeded. In due time it was extended to France, Germany, Italy, Belgium, Holland, Norway, Sweden, Switzerland, and Denmark.

Some of the newspapers in America were doubtful of the merits of the Hero Fund and the first annual report was criticized, but all this has passed away and the action of the fund is now warmly extolled. It has conquered, and long will it be before the trust is allowed to perish!

The Hero Fund will prove chiefly a pension fund. Already it has many pensioners, heroes or the widows or children of heroes. A strange misconception arose at first about it. Many thought that its purpose was to stimulate heroic action, that heroes were to be induced to play their parts for the sake of reward. This never entered my mind. It is absurd. True heroes think not of reward. They are inspired and think only of their fellows endangered; never of themselves. The fund is intended to pension or provide in the most suitable manner for the hero should he be disabled, or for those dependent upon him should he perish in his attempt to save others.

CHAPTER XVI

HELP FOR THE COLLEGES

THE fifteen-million-dollar pension fund for aged university professors, the Carnegie Endowment for the Advancement of Learning, the fourth important gift, given in June, 1905, is very near and dear to me—knowing, as I do, many who are soon to become beneficiaries, and convinced as I am of their worth and the value of the service already rendered by them. To save for old age with these men is impossible. Hence the universities without pension funds are compelled to retain men who are no longer able, should no longer be required, to perform their duties. Of the usefulness of the fund no doubt can be entertained. The first list of beneficiaries published was conclusive upon this point, containing as it did several names of world-wide reputation, so great had been their contributions to the stock of human knowledge. Many of these beneficiaries and their widows have written me most affecting letters. These I can never destroy, for if I ever have a fit of melancholy, I know the cure lies in re-reading these letters.

My friend, Mr. Thomas Shaw (now Lord Shaw), of Dunfermline, had written an article for one of the English reviews showing that many poor people in Scotland were unable to pay the fees required to give their children a university education, although some had deprived themselves of comforts in order to do so. After reading Mr. Shaw's article the idea came to me to give ten millions in five per cent bonds, one half of the £104,000 yearly revenue from it to be used to pay the fees of the deserving poor students and the other half to improve the universities.

My election to the Lord Rectorship of St. Andrews in 1902 proved a very important event in my life. It admitted me to the university world, to which I had been a stranger. Few incidents in my life have so deeply impressed me as the first meeting of the faculty, when I took my seat in the old chair occupied successively by so many distinguished Lord Rectors during the nearly five hundred years which have elapsed since St. Andrews was founded.

An invitation given to the principals of the four Scotch universities and their wives or daughters to spend a week at Skibo resulted in much joy to Mrs. Carnegie and myself. After that "Principals' Week" each year became an established custom. They as well as we became friends, and thereby, they all agree, great good results to the universities. A spirit of coöperation is stimulated. Taking my hand upon leaving after the first yearly visit, Principal Lang said: "It has taken the principals of the Scotch universities five hundred years to learn how to begin our sessions. Spending a week together is the solution."

My unanimous reëlection by the students of St. Andrews, without a contest for a second term, was deeply appreciated. And I like the Rector's nights, when the students claim him for themselves, no member of the faculty being invited. We always had a good time. After the first one, Principal Donaldson gave me the verdict of the Secretary as rendered to him: "Rector So-and-So talked *to* us, Rector Thus-and-so talked *at* us, both from the platform; Mr. Carnegie sat down in our circle and talked *with* us."

The question of aid to our own higher educational

institutions often intruded itself upon me, but my belief was that our chief universities, such as Harvard and Columbia, with five to ten thousand students, were large enough; that further growth was undesirable; that the smaller institutions (the colleges especially) were in greater need of help and that it would be a better use of surplus wealth to aid them. Accordingly, I afterwards confined myself to these and am satisfied that this was wise.

My connection with Hampton and Tuskegee Institutes, which promote the elevation of the colored race we formerly kept in slavery, has been a source of satisfaction and pleasure, and to know Booker Washington is a rare privilege. We should all take our hats off to the man who not only raised himself from slavery, but helped raise millions of his race to a higher stage of civilization. Mr. Washington called upon me a few days after my gift of six hundred thousand dollars was made to Tuskegee and asked if he might be allowed to make one suggestion. I said: "Certainly."

"You have kindly specified that a sum from that fund be set aside for the future support of myself and wife during our lives, and we are very grateful, but, Mr. Carnegie, the sum is far beyond our needs and will seem to my race a fortune. Some might feel that I was no longer a poor man giving my services without thought of saving money. Would you have any objection to changing that clause, striking out the sum, and substituting 'only suitable provision'? I'll trust the trustees. Mrs. Washington and myself need very little."

I did so, and the deed now stands, but when Mr. Baldwin asked for the original letter to exchange it for the substitute, he told me that the noble soul objected. That document addressed to him was to be preserved forever, and handed down; but he would put it aside and let the substitute go on file.

This is an indication of the character of the leader of his race. No truer, more self-sacrificing hero ever lived: a man compounded of all the virtues. It makes one better just to know such pure and noble souls—human nature in its highest types is already divine here on earth. If it be asked which man of our age, or even of the past ages, has risen from the lowest to the highest, the answer must be Booker Washington. He rose from slavery to the leadership of his people—a modern Moses and Joshua combined, leading his people both onward and upward.

My giving of organs to churches came very early in my career, I having presented to less than a hundred members of the Swedenborgian Church in Allegheny which my father favored, an organ. Applications from other churches soon began to pour in, from the grand Catholic Cathedral of Pittsburgh down to the small church in the country village, and I was kept busy. Every church seemed to need a better organ than it had, and as the full price for the new instrument was paid, what the old one brought was clear profit. Some ordered organs for very small churches which would almost split the rafters, as was the case with the first organ given the Swedenborgians; others had bought organs before applying but our check to cover the amount was welcome. Finally, however, a rigid system of giving was developed. A printed schedule requiring answers to many questions has now to be filled and returned before action is taken. The department is now perfectly systematized and works admirably because we graduate the gift according to the size of the church.

Of all my work of a philanthropic character, my

private pension fund gives me the highest and noblest return. No satisfaction equals that of feeling you have been permitted to place in comfortable circumstances, in their old age, people whom you have long known to be kind and good and in every way deserving, but who, from no fault of their own, have not sufficient means to live respectably, free from solicitude as to their mere maintenance. Modest sums insure this freedom. It surprised me to find how numerous were those who needed some aid to make the difference between an old age of happiness and one of misery. Some such cases had arisen before my retirement from business, and I had sweet satisfaction from this source. Not one person have I ever placed upon the pension list that did not fully deserve assistance. It is a real roll of honor and mutual affection. All are worthy. There is no publicity about it. No one knows who is embraced. Not a word is ever breathed to others.

The Railroad Pension Fund is of a similar nature. Many of the old boys of the Pittsburgh Division (or their widows) are taken care of by it. It began years ago and grew to its present proportions. It now benefits the worthy railroad men who served under me when I was superintendent on the Pennsylvania, or their widows, who need help. I was only a boy when I first went among these trainmen and got to know them by name. They were very kind to me. Most of the men beneficiaries of the fund I have known personally. They are dear friends.

Although the four-million-dollar fund I gave for workmen in the mills (Steel Workers' Pensions) embraces hundreds that I never saw, there are still a sufficient number upon it that I do remember to give that fund also a strong hold upon me.

CHAPTER XVII

HAIL, LAIRD OF PITTENCRIEFF

PEACE, at least as between English-speaking peoples, must have been early in my thoughts. In 1869, when Britain launched the monster *Monarch*, then the largest warship known, there was, for some now-forgotten reason, talk of how she could easily compel tribute from our American cities one after the other. Nothing could resist her. I cabled John Bright, then in the British Cabinet (the cable had recently been opened):

"First and best service possible for Monarch, bringing home body Peabody."

No signature was given. Strange to say, this was done, and thus the *Monarch* became the messenger of peace, not of destruction. Many years afterwards I met Mr. Bright at a small dinner party in Birmingham and told him I was his young anonymous correspondent. He was surprised that no signature was attached and said his heart was in the act. I am sure it was. He is entitled to all credit.

I became interested in the Peace Society of Great Britain upon one of my early visits and attended many of its meetings. The abolition of war grew in importance with me until it finally overshadowed all other issues. The surprising action of the first Hague Conference gave me intense joy. Called primarily to consider disarmament (which proved a dream), it created the commanding reality of a permanent tribunal to settle international disputes. I saw in this the greatest step toward peace that humanity had ever taken, and taken as if by inspiration, without much previous discussion. No wonder the sublime idea captivated the conference.

When Andrew D. White and Mr. Holls, upon their return from The Hague, suggested that I offer the funds needed for a Temple of Peace at The Hague, I informed them that I never could be so presumptuous; that if the Government of the Netherlands informed me of its desire to have such a temple and hoped I would furnish the means, the request would be favorably considered. They demurred, saying this could hardly be expected from any Government. Then I said I could never act in the matter.

Finally the Dutch Government did make application, through its Minister, Baron Gevers in Washington, and I rejoiced. Still, in writing him, I was careful to say that the drafts of his Government would be duly honored. I did not send the money. The Government drew upon me for it, and the draft for a million and a half is kept as a memento. It seems to me almost too much that any individual should be permitted to perform so noble a duty as that of providing means for this Temple of Peace—the most holy building in the world because it has the holiest end in view.

When in 1907 friends came and asked me to accept the presidency of the Peace Society of New York, which they had determined to organize, I declined, alleging that I was kept very busy with many affairs, which was true; but my conscience troubled me afterwards for declining. If I were not willing to sacrifice myself for the cause of peace what should I sacrifice for? What was I good for? Fortunately, in a few days, the Reverend Lyman Abbott, the Reverend Mr. Lynch, and some other notable laborers for good causes called to urge my reconsideration. I divined their errand and frankly told them they need not speak. My conscience had been tormenting me for declining and I would accept the presidency and do my duty. After that came the great national gathering (the following April) when for the first time in the history of Peace Society meetings, there attended delegates from thirty-five of the states of the Union, besides many foreigners of distinction.

No gift I have made or can ever make can possibly approach that of Pittencrieff Glen, Dunfermline. It is saturated with childish sentiment—all of the purest and sweetest. I must tell that story:

Among my earliest recollections are the struggles of Dunfermline to obtain the rights of the town to part of the Abbey grounds and the Palace ruins. My Grandfather Morrison began the campaign, or, at least, was one of those who did. The struggle was continued by my Uncles Lauder and Morrison, the latter honored by being charged with having incited and led a band of men to tear down a certain wall. The citizens won a victory in the highest court and the then Laird ordered that thereafter "no Morrison be admitted to the Glen." I, being a Morrison like my brother-cousin, Dod, was debarred. The Lairds of Pittencrieff for generations had been at variance with the inhabitants.

The Glen is unique, as far as I know. It adjoins the Abbey and Palace grounds, and on the west and north it lies along two of the main streets of the town. Its area (between sixty and seventy acres) is finely sheltered, its high hills grandly wooded. It always meant paradise to the child of Dunfermline. It certainly did to me. When I heard of paradise, I translated the word into Pittencrieff Glen, believing it to be as near to paradise as anything I could think of. Happy were we if through an open lodge gate, or over the wall or under the iron grill over the burn, now and then we caught a glimpse inside.

Almost every Sunday Uncle Lauder took "Dod" and "Naig" for a walk around the Abbey to a part that overlooked the Glen—the busy crows fluttering around in the big trees below. Its Laird was to us children the embodiment of rank and wealth. The Queen, we knew, lived in Windsor Castle, but she didn't own Pittencrieff, not she! Hunt of Pittencrieff wouldn't exchange with her or with any one. Of this we were sure, because certainly neither of us would. In all my childhood's—yes, and in my early manhood's—air-castle building (which was not small), nothing comparable in grandeur approached Pittencrieff. My Uncle Lauder predicted many things for me when I became a man, but had he foretold that some day I should be rich enough, and so supremely fortunate as to become Laird of Pittencrieff, he might have turned my head. And then to be able to hand it over to Dunfermline as a public park—my paradise of childhood! Not for a crown would I barter that privilege.

When Dr. Ross whispered to me that Colonel Hunt might be induced to sell, my ears cocked themselves instantly. He wished an extortionate price, the doctor thought, and I heard nothing further for some time. When indisposed in London in the autumn of 1902, my mind ran upon the subject, and I intended to wire Dr. Ross to come up and see me. One morning, Mrs. Carnegie came into my room and asked me to guess who had arrived and I guessed Dr. Ross. Sure enough, there he was. We talked over Pittencrieff. I suggested that if our mutual friend and fellow-townsman, Mr.

Shaw in Edinburgh (Lord Shaw of Dunfermline), ever met Colonel Hunt's agents he could intimate that their client might some day regret not closing with me as another purchaser equally anxious to buy might not be met with, and I might change my mind or pass away. Mr. Shaw told the doctor when he mentioned this that he had an appointment to meet with Hunt's lawyer on other business the next morning and would certainly say so.

I sailed shortly after for New York and received there one day a cable from Mr. Shaw stating that the Laird would accept forty-five thousand pounds. Should he close? I wired: "Yes, provided it is under Ross's conditions"; and on Christmas Eve, I received Shaw's reply: "Hail, Laird of Pittencrieff!" So I was the happy possessor of the grandest title on earth in my estimation. The King—well, he was only the King. He didn't own King Malcolm's Tower nor St. Margaret's Shrine, nor Pittencrieff Glen. Not he, poor man. I did, and I shall be glad to condescendingly show the King those treasures should he ever visit Dunfermline.

As the possessor of the Park and the Glen I had a chance to find out what, if anything, money could do for the good of the masses of a community, if placed in the hands of a body of public-spirited citizens. Dr. Ross was taken into my confidence so far as Pittencrieff Park was concerned, and with his advice certain men intended for a body of trustees were agreed upon and invited to Skibo to organize. They imagined it was in regard to transferring the Park to the town; not even to Dr. Ross was any other subject mentioned. When they heard that half a million sterling in bonds, bearing five per cent interest, was also to go to them for the benefit of Dunfermline, they were surprised.

It is twelve years since the Glen was handed over to the trustees and certainly no public park was ever dearer to a people. The children's yearly gala day, the flower shows and the daily use of the Park by the people are surprising. The Glen now attracts people from neighboring towns. In numerous ways the trustees have succeeded finely in the direction indicated in the trust deed, namely:

"To bring into the monotonous lives of the toiling masses of Dunfermline, more 'of sweetness and light,' to give to them—especially the young—some charm, some happiness, some elevating conditions of life which residence elsewhere would have denied, that the child of my native town, looking back in after years, however far from home it may have roamed, will feel that simply by virtue of being such, life has been made happier and better. If this be the fruit of your labors, you will have succeeded; if not, you will have failed."

Thus, Pittencrieff Glen is the most soul-satisfying public gift I ever made, or ever can make. It is poetic justice that the grandson of Thomas Morrison, radical leader in his day, nephew of Bailie Morrison, his son and successor, and above all son of my sainted father and my most heroic mother, should arise and dispossess the lairds, should become the agent for conveying the Glen and Park to the people of Dunfermline forever. It is a true romance, which no air-castle can quite equal or fiction conceive. The hand of destiny seems to hover over it, and I hear something whispering: "Not altogether in vain have you lived—not altogether in vain." This is the crowning mercy of my career! I set it apart from all my other public gifts. Truly the whirligig of time brings in some strange revenges.

It is now thirteen years since I ceased to accumulate

wealth and began to distribute it. I could never have succeeded in either had I stopped with having enough to retire upon, but nothing to retire to. But there was the habit and the love of reading, writing and speaking upon occasion, and also the acquaintance and friendship of educated men which I had made before I gave up business. For some years after retiring I could not force myself to visit the works. This, alas, would recall so many who had gone before. Scarcely one of my early friends would remain to give me the hand-clasp of the days of old. Only one or two of these old men would call me "Andy."

Do not let it be thought, however, that my younger partners were forgotten, or that they have not played a very important part in sustaining me in the effort of reconciling myself to the new conditions. Far otherwise! The most soothing influence of all was their prompt organization of the Carnegie Veteran Association, to expire only when the last member dies. Our yearly dinner together, in our own home in New York, is a source of the greatest pleasure,—so great that it lasts from one year to the other. Some of the Veterans travel far to be present, and what occurs between us constitutes one of the dearest joys of my life. I carry with me the affection of "my boys." I am certain I do. There is no possible mistake about that because my heart goes out to them. This I number among my many blessings and in many a brooding hour this fact comes to me, and I say to myself: "Rather this, minus fortune, than multimillionairedom without it—yes, a thousand times, yes."

Many friends, great and good men and women, Mrs. Carnegie and I are favored to know, but not one whit shall these ever change our joint love for the "boys."

For to my infinite delight her heart goes out to them as does mine. She it was who christened our new New York home with the first Veteran dinner. "The partners first" was her word. It was no mere idle form when they elected Mrs. Carnegie the first honorary member, and our daughter the second. Their place in our hearts is secure. Although I was the senior, still we were "boys together." Perfect trust and common aims, not for self only, but for each other, and deep affection, moulded us into a brotherhood. We were friends first and partners afterwards. Forty-three out of forty-five partners are thus bound together for life.

. . . .

Mr. Carnegie was happily jotting down his recollections of earlier days and entering lightly and cheerfully upon the first years of his old age, when the World War broke out, a crushing blow to the lover of peace. Illness and feebleness came swiftly upon him; but the evening of his life was gentle and kindly, brightened, even amid the horrors of warfare, by the hope that the world would yet see good arising from the evil. In 1919 he died. Of these last years his wife wrote that he was "always patient, considerate, cheerful, grateful for any little pleasure or service, never thinking of himself, but always of the dawning of the better day."

Amina's Blanket

HELEN DUNMORE

Illustrated by

JUDITH LAWTON

HEINEMANN • LONDON

William Heinemann Ltd
A division of Reed Children's Books
Michelin House
81 Fulham Road London SW3 6RB
and Auckland, Melbourne, Singapore and Toronto

First published 1996

ISBN 0 434 96947 8

Produced by Mandarin Offset Ltd
Printed and bound in China

A school pack of BANANA BOOKS 85-90 is
available from Heinemann Educational Books
ISBN 0 435 00083 7

CHAPTER 1

'JOSIE!' MISS HEATHER'S voice cracked across the classroom. Josie jumped.

'Dreaming again!' scolded Miss Heather. 'Well, you nearly missed something very exciting.'

But Josie couldn't believe that anything exciting was going to happen at ten o'clock on a wet Monday morning in Miss Heather's class.

'Right!' said Miss Heather. 'Wait two minutes and I'll bring it in.'

Then she went out with a mysterious smile, leaving the door open. What was she talking about? Josie stared across the table at Natasha.

'Blankets!' mouthed Natasha. If she talked out loud, Rosie Gold would tell on her.

'*Blankets*?' whispered Josie. 'What do you mean?'

But just at that moment Miss Heather swished back into the classroom with a big, bulgy, black plastic rubbish bag. She put it down on the table next to Josie, and began to untie the string round the neck of the bag. Rosie Gold pushed forward to

help her. The black bag wobbled on the table as if there was something alive inside it. Then the string was undone and colour poured out like rain. Red and gold and orange and sparkling silver. Midnight blue and kingfisher blue and a white as fluffy as a field of snow in the sunlight. There was forest green and warm, buttery yellow and a rainbow ball like a patch of oil on the

road after rain. The colours met and danced as they rolled out over the table.

'There!' said Miss Heather. 'Look what Mr Stassinopolous has given us for our blanket! Isn't it kind of him? Now, if each of you takes one ball of wool, and knits one square, we can sew them all up and make a beautiful warm blanket.'

Josie put up her hand. 'Please, Miss, who's the blanket for?'

'Josie, you weren't listening at all, were you? Now, can someone tell her?'

Rosie Gold's hand wagged in the air, but for once Miss Heather did not choose her. She chose Jason Connolly.

'It's a blanket for someone who lives in a city where there's war. For an old person who hasn't got any heating.'

'Or a child,' chipped in Natasha.

'That's right, Jason,' said Miss Heather. 'Our blanket is going to go far away to the country I showed you on the map. It will go to help someone keep warm through the hard winter. Lots of houses and flats have been damaged by shells because of the war. People are homeless.'

'Shells . . . ' whispered Josie dreamily, thinking of the glisten of sea-shells on the sand when the tide was out. 'How can shells damage a house?'

'It's not that sort of shell. These shells explode, like bombs. They break walls and windows. They kill people,' said Natasha, who always listened when Miss Heather was talking.

'Oh,' said Josie. Then she put her hand up.

'Yes, Josie?' said Miss Heather.

'Is it snowing there, where the war is?' asked Josie.

'It snows there all winter long,' said Miss Heather, 'and often it's too dangerous for people to go out and gather wood to light fires. They get very cold.'

'Why don't they turn on the central

heating then?' sniggered Darren Fox.

'They don't have central heating there, stupid!' Rosie Gold told him. Miss Heather looked sad.

'Oh yes, they do,' she said. 'They used to have nice flats with central heating, just like you, before the war. But the bombs and shells have destroyed them. Now, let's give this out. One ball of wool each.'

'I ought to have the gold,' said Rosie Gold, 'like my name, Miss.' Everyone wanted the gold, but Rosie got it. A crowd of hands snatched and pulled at the balls of wool. Then, suddenly, they were all gone except for a ball of dark blue that was a bit smaller than the others. Josie picked it up and squeezed its warm softness.

'It's not fair. Yours is the smallest,' said Natasha.

'I like it,' said Josie, and she did.

Miss Heather drew a square on the board and showed them how many stitches they had to do. They were allowed to take the wool home to do their knitting.

'I want this blanket finished by the end of the week!' said Miss Heather. 'Thirty beautiful squares.'

CHAPTER 2

AT HOME JOSIE knitted and knitted. Sometimes a hole came in her square and Mum had to help her pick up the stitches she had dropped. For a long time there was only a little wiggly strip of knitting on her needles, then suddenly her square started to grow.

'If I do six more rows tonight, it'll be finished,' she said to Mum on Wednesday. Her square looked like a little patch of midnight sky. Josie stroked it and wondered who would get the blanket. Would they like her blue square as much as she did?

That night Josie finished her square. She was not the only one. At school next morning the tables were covered with finished blanket squares. Red and gold and kingfisher blue and ebony black and green as bright as grass in summer. There was white like a corner of a snowy field, and a patch like the midnight sky. Miss Heather counted the squares.

'Thirty!' she said happily. 'Well done, Class Five. Now, all we've got to do is get the squares sewn up into a blanket.' She looked worried. 'But I don't know if I'll have the time to do it. There's a staff meeting this evening.'

Josie's hand shot up before anyone else's. 'My Mum'll do it!' she called out. 'She's really good at sewing.'

'Are you sure, Josie? Well, that would be a great help. If we fold all the squares and put them back in the sack, can you manage to carry it home?'

'Yes, of course,' said Josie.

Mum looked surprised when Josie tipped the bundle of squares onto the living room carpet. For a moment Josie thought she was going to be cross, but she wasn't.

'But you'll have to help, Josie. I can't do all this on my own,' she said.

First Mum ironed the squares, then they took thin wool and fat needles and started to sew them together. Josie sewed one strip of five squares, and Mum sewed another. Josie sewed and sewed until her fingers were sore from pushing the needle through the wool.

All the time she thought about the person in the cold faraway city who would get the blanket. It was very late and all the colours of the rainbow were dancing in front of Josie's eyes.

'Thanks, Josie. You go to bed now. I'll finish this,' said Mum.

When Josie was nearly asleep, Mum brought in the finished blanket. She spread it out on top of Josie's duvet. It was the most beautiful blanket in the world.

'Can I keep it here, just for tonight?' asked Josie.

'Yes, just for tonight,' said Mum.

Josie slept. Mum went to bed and the sky was as dark as the square of midnight blue Josie had knitted.

CHAPTER 3

A NOISE LIKE thunder woke Josie. She sat up and clutched the blanket. It felt warm and soft in her fingers, but the room had gone very cold. Josie shivered and pulled the blanket tight round her. The thunder rumbled again, and the room shook. Through the window Josie saw a patch of midnight sky, then a flash like lightning.

'Mum!' she whispered. She was too frightened to shout.

There was a rustling sound on the other side of the room, then a voice answered. But it wasn't Mum's voice. And the room didn't look like Josie's bedroom any more.

'Hello,' the voice said. 'Who are you?'

'Josie,' whispered Josie.

'Did the shells destroy your flat? Are you looking for shelter?' asked the voice. It sounded friendly. Josie peered round the room and saw a dark bundle on the floor, against the wall. She wrapped the blanket tight round her and tiptoed across to it. The floor felt like ice under her bare feet.

'You sound scared. You can stay here with me if you want, Josie,' said the voice.

Bright flashes like lightning lit the room. Josie saw that the bundle was a girl, curled up to keep warm. She was about the same age as Josie, and she had long dark hair, like Josie's.

Suddenly there was a terrible bang and the floor shook. Josie tripped up and fell onto the floor next to the girl.

'That shell came close,' said the girl. 'I hope it didn't hit any of my friends'

flats. Oooh, what's that you've got? It's nice and warm and soft.'

'It's a blanket,' said Josie. 'You can put half of it over you if you want.' Josie wriggled close to the girl and spread the blanket over them both. There was another bang and the wall trembled behind Josie's back.

'It's all right,' said the girl. 'That shell wasn't so close.'

'What's your name?' asked Josie.

'Amina.'

'Are you all on your own?'

'No,' said Amina. 'I've got a friend here. Give me your hand.' Amina took Josie's hand. 'Here, feel,' said Amina. Josie felt something soft and warm in Amina's hand. It was even softer than the blanket.

'Stroke him,' said Amina. 'He won't bite you.'

The something soft and warm was alive. It wriggled under Josie's fingers. 'What is it? A hamster?' asked Josie.

'No, he's my pet mouse. He used to be wild, but I tamed him. He's called Sinta. Only you mustn't tell, because food is so short and Mum won't let me give him anything.'

'Where's your Mum?'

'She went out to get wood, before it got dark,' said Amina. 'Only then they started shelling. As soon as they stop, she'll come back. She always does.' But Josie felt Amina shivering. How cold and frightened she must be, lying alone on the floor all night, waiting for her Mum to come home with wood to light a fire.

'You can have more of the blanket if you want. I'm not cold,' said Josie, and she tucked the blanket in round Amina.

'Poor little Sinta, I haven't got anything for you tonight,' said Amina. 'You'll have to wait till Mum gets back.'

'What does he eat?' asked Josie.

Amina laughed. 'The same as me!' she said. 'He hides in my pocket and has a little bit of whatever Mum brings back.' There was a soft squeak from Sinta.

'He knows we're talking about food,' said Amina. 'Where did you get this blanket, Josie? It must be the softest one in the city. It's even warmer than a fire.'

'You should see the colours!' said Josie. 'It's all made of squares of different colours. The one I knitted is dark blue, just the same colour as that patch of sky in the window.'

'I like it when the sky is dark blue, with no shell flashes,' said Amina. 'That means it's safe. Tell me more about the colours. Everything's so grey and dirty in the city now.'

'Well, there's a white like fluffy snow –' began Josie.

'Brrr, don't talk about snow! You'll make me feel cold again!'

'OK,' said Josie, and she tried to think of colours which would make Amina feel warm. 'There's yellow and red like the sun when it's going down on a holiday evening in summer.

There's green like the shade of the trees when we sit under them in dinner hour. There's –'

Suddenly the window was full of a blinding white light. A second later the room rocked. A crash like a thousand storms ripped through the building. It picked up Josie and Amina and threw them across the room.

There was a terrible rumbling as if the building were falling apart, and the starlit sky showed where the window had once been. Josie's mouth was full of dust and smoke. She coughed and choked. The blanket was gone, Amina was gone, Sinta was gone. She could smell burning. How close was it? Was it in the building?

CHAPTER 4

'AMINA!' JOSIE WHISPERED. She couldn't shout because of all the dust.

'Josie!' came a little croaky voice from under the window.

'What happened? Did something hit us?'

'It was close. The closest we've had.'

'Is there a fire?'

The light in the window was changing

to red. Amina got up and peered out. 'There's a fire just down the street,' she told Josie. Josie picked herself up off the floor and stumbled over to Amina. She saw long red flames licking out of a block of flats, and people, like black ants, running in the streets. Fire leapt into the sky, changing it from dark-blue to orange.

It was nearly as light as day.

'Poor Sinta,' said Amina. 'He's so frightened of shells. He's afraid we'll get hit.'

'Where is he?'

'In my pocket, right down at the bottom. Can you feel him?' Josie felt the little shivering mouse, deep in Amina's pocket. The walls of Amina's room were shivering too.

'The fire is spreading,' said Amina. 'It's coming this way. I wish Mum was here.'

The fire crackled and rushed. It sounded as if it was nearly in the room. Then Josie and Amina heard voices shouting. The voices were coming nearer and nearer.

'Rescuers!' said Amina. 'They're coming to get us out!'

The fire was coming closer. Which

would get to them first, the fire or the rescuers? Josie grabbed Amina's hand and they stumbled to the broken doorway. There was so much smoke that their eyes hurt. Josie coughed when she tried to breathe, and the fire roared like a lion outside. Suddenly the rescuers' voices were loud, just on the other side of the door.

'We're in here!' shouted Amina.

CHAPTER 5

THE DOOR FLEW open. Josie blinked as the bright sun chased across her bed. Mum was pulling back the curtains.

'Come on, Josie, you'll be late for school,' said Mum, 'and you've got to take that blanket in, remember.'

Josie felt on the bed for the blanket. It was there, as bright and beautiful as ever, all the colours of the rainbow.

'Amina!' whispered Josie. Where was Amina? Josie picked up the blanket. It smelled of smoke and danger. It smelled of war. Where was Amina now?

Miss Heather packed the blanket up in a parcel and sent it away. Weeks passed. Everybody had forgotten about the blanket, except Josie. But one day Miss Heather came into the classroom waving a big brown envelope.

'Class Five!' she said. 'We've had a letter about our blanket. And some photographs.'

Miss Heather rustled in the envelope and held up a big photograph.

'Look,' she said. 'These are the people who have lost their homes because of the war. Their houses were shelled, and now they're in a centre for homeless people. If you look carefully,

you can see the blankets on their beds. One of them is the blanket we made.'

The photograph showed a crowd of people huddled together in a big hall. There was a row of beds with blankets on them. And by one of the beds, there was a girl, about Josie's age, with long dark hair. Josie stared. Surely she knew that face. Josie could not stay in her chair. She had to get closer to the photograph.

'Josie!' said Miss Heather. But Josie was staring at the face of the dark-haired girl.

'Amina!' she whispered. 'It's Amina! The girl in my dream!'

It *was* Amina in the photograph. And one hand was in her pocket. Josie knew she was stroking Sinta.

'Sit down, Josie!' said Miss Heather crossly, and Josie had to sit down.

'Our blanket is on one of those beds,' said Miss Heather.

But Josie knew it was on Amina's bed. *Amina isn't a dream*, she thought, *she's a real girl. My dream was real. Amina had to leave her home because of the shelling and the fire.*

The blanket was on Amina's bed in the centre for homeless people. All the colours of the rainbow were there. The red, the gold, the orange, the forest green, the snowy white and the midnight blue that Josie had knitted. The blanket would wrap round Amina at night and keep her warm.

'Sleep well, Amina,' said Josie, so softly that no-one heard her.